CW01640760

GUILD

TUTOR ASSESSMENT PACK

ENGLISH

YEAR 6

Pearson

Tutora

CONTENTS

CONTENTS

How to use this pack

This *Tutors' Guild* Year 6 English Tutor Assessment Pack is full of assessment opportunities to help you prepare your student for the Key Stage 2 national curriculum tests. You can keep a record of your student's achievements using the progress tracker on pages 9–10. Everything in this pack is available for you to download as an editable file. This means that every test can be edited to suit the needs of an individual student, but also that you can print off each resource as many times as you need.

Types of test

The pack comprises three types of test, detailed below.

Checkpoint challenges

These tests are designed to each assess one subject area from the English curriculum: Reading; Writing; Grammar and punctuation; Spelling. The challenges will take around an hour, but needn't be strictly timed.

Each challenge will cover content taught during the corresponding lessons in the *Tutors' Guild* Year 6 English Tutor Delivery Pack (ISBN 978 1 292 17251 4). Checkpoint challenges are not designed to be exam-style but the content they cover is taken from the content domain of the English reading and grammar, punctuation and spelling test frameworks (see pages 7–10 of the Tutor Delivery Pack for more on the English curriculum). The challenges replicate the style of the Tutor Delivery Pack activity sheets: familiar, unintimidating and engaging.

Checkpoint challenges can be used at any time during the course of tutoring – as a diagnostic at the beginning of the year or as revision before the tests, for example – but the most useful time to use them is at the end of each subject area as a summative test of your student's knowledge. The challenge may reveal an area in which your student lacks confidence and assessment throughout the year gives you plenty of time to address those areas.

There is a set of answers for every checkpoint challenge, with guidance on mark allocation where appropriate, at the back of this pack.

Topic tests

For every lesson in the Tutor Delivery Pack, there is a topic test. These shorter tests each have ten marks and should take around 20 minutes to complete. They have the same friendly, accessible look as the Tutor Delivery Pack activity sheets, in order to make assessment much less stressful for your student while allowing you to regularly and effectively track progress.

As with every aspect of the *Tutors' Guild* series, topic tests are designed to be completely flexible. Tutors with more than an hour per lesson may choose to complete the test at the end of the lesson or at the beginning of the next, to test knowledge retention. Equally, the tests are short enough that they can be given to students to complete during the week, instead of or alongside the suggested homework activity for the lesson. You may also wish to use the topic tests to revisit topics with which your student struggled when completing the checkpoint challenges or practice papers.

Answers to all tests are provided at the back of this pack.

Practice papers

In order to successfully prepare your student for the Key Stage 2 national curriculum tests, you should ensure they have the chance to experience 'exam-style' assessment. The practice papers in this pack give your student the perfect opportunity to become accustomed to the layout and demands of the national curriculum tests. For more on the content and style of the tests, see pages 7–8.

To get the most out of the practice papers, you may wish to have your student complete them well in advance of the test. This will ensure you have time to address any difficulties that may become apparent. As there are three papers, it is advisable to complete them over a period of several weeks, so as not to put your student under too much pressure.

Answers and mark schemes are provided at the back of this pack.

How to use this pack

Progress tracking

On pages 9–10 of this pack, you will find a progress tracker to fill in every time your student completes an assessment. There is space on the tracker for you to record a first and second attempt at each test, if you wish to do so. When your student completes a test, look closely at the results and try to pick out patterns in their mistakes. Make a note of these patterns in the areas to work on column so that you can use your future contact time together most effectively. You may wish to fill in the *talk about the test* page (page 11) with your student to find out which questions they found the hardest to answer, particularly if the test doesn't reveal much because your student didn't get many questions wrong.

Information for parents

The information for parents provided on pages 5–6 of this pack is very similar to that in the Tutor Delivery Pack. This has been repeated for tutors who have decided to purchase one of the packs but not the other. If the parents of your student have seen the information in the Tutor Delivery Pack, you may just wish to explain the different types of test to them.

Certificates

In the digital version of this pack, you will find two customisable certificates. These can be edited to celebrate achievements throughout the year.

INFORMATION FOR PARENTS

INTRODUCTION

Your child's tutor will often make use of resources from the *Tutors' Guild* Year 6 English series. These resources fit perfectly with the current national curriculum tests. The tutor will use their expert knowledge and judgement to assess your child's current needs. This will allow them to target areas for improvement, build confidence levels and develop skills as quickly as possible, giving your child the chance to succeed in the end of Key Stage 2 tests or in their Year 7 resits.

Just as a classroom teacher might do, your tutor will use practice papers and tests to prepare your child for the new national curriculum tests, formerly known as SATs. Each set of resources has been designed by experts in primary English and reviewed by experienced classroom teachers and tutors to ensure it offers great quality, effective and enjoyable assessment. All *Tutors' Guild* resources are fully flexible and adaptable so that your tutor can tailor the course to meet your child's needs.

TYPES OF TEST

Checkpoint challenge

Checkpoint challenges are designed to test your child's knowledge of a whole area of English. There are four challenges: one in reading, one in writing, one in grammar and punctuation and one in spelling. The challenges are child-friendly in design, while still testing the topics your child will come across in the national curriculum test.

Your tutor may decide to complete the challenges during teaching time. This may depend on your child's confidence levels or reading ability, or it may be that they want to assess your child more informally and to discuss the challenge while completing it. Otherwise, your tutor will give your child the challenge to complete for homework. Each challenge will take around an hour.
If your child is completing the challenge for homework, you don't need to time them strictly.

Topic tests

Topic tests are short, 20-minute tests that are worth ten marks each. They are designed to be fun and unintimidating for your child. They test much smaller areas (topics) of English. Whereas there is a checkpoint challenge testing all reading skills, there are individual topic tests for each skill: finding answers, making comparisons and so on. There are 38 topic tests in total, which is enough for one per school week. Again, if your child completes a test for homework, you do not need to time their completion.

Practice papers

The *practice papers* replicate the tests that your child will sit at the end of Year 6. See page 6 for a breakdown of these tests. If your child is given a practice paper, you may want to provide a quiet environment and time it more strictly so their experience of the paper is closer to 'the real thing'.

FURTHER SUPPORT FOR YOUR CHILD

Parents often ask a tutor what else they can do to support their child's learning or what resources they can buy to provide extra revision and practice. As a Pearson resource, *Tutors' Guild* has been designed to complement the popular *Revise* series. Useful titles you may wish to purchase include:

- *Revise* KS2 SATs English Revision Guide – Expected Standard (ISBN 978 12921 460 10)
- *Revise* KS2 SATs English Revision Workbook – Expected Standard (ISBN 978 12921 460 03)
- *Revise* KS2 SATs English Practice Papers (ISBN 978 12921 459 76)
- *Revise* KS2 SATs English – Grammar – Targeted Practice (ISBN 978 12921 459 45)
- *Revise* KS2 SATs English – Reading Comprehension – Targeted Practice (ISBN 978 12921 459 52)
- *Revise* KS2 SATs English – Spelling – Targeted Practice (ISBN 978 12921 459 69)

'Above expected standard' editions of the Revision Guide and Revision Workbook are available.

INFORMATION FOR PARENTS

WHAT'S IN THE TEST?

You may have heard a lot about the new national curriculum tests from your child's school, from other parents or in the media. Here is a breakdown of the tests that your child will sit at the end of Year 6.

GRAMMAR, PUNCTUATION AND SPELLING (GPS)

Your child will sit two tests that assess grammar, punctuation and spelling ability:

Paper 1: questions
This is a 45-minute test in which your child will be given 49 questions to answer on grammar, punctuation and vocabulary. Some answers will be non-verbal (tick boxes) and some will be verbal (written words and sentences).

Paper 2: spelling
The spelling test is administered by a teacher and as such is not strictly timed. It consists of 20 words that your child will have to spell correctly. Each spelling is read aloud by the teacher several times and your child will be given a sentence in which to put the word. This will give your child the chance to think about the word in context.

READING

Your child will sit only one test to assess their reading ability. However, they will also be assessed by their classroom teacher throughout the year.

Paper 1: English reading test
This test is one hour long, including reading time. Your child will be given a reading booklet with a selection of texts: non-fiction, stories and poetry. They will also be given an answer booklet which will have a number of comprehension questions worth 50 marks in total. Your child will have to answer all of the questions about each of the texts. As with GPS paper 1, some answers will be non-verbal (tick boxes) and some will be verbal (written words and sentences).

WRITING

Year 6 students no longer sit a writing test at the end of the year. Instead, your child's writing abilities will be assessed throughout the year by their classroom teacher. Their teacher will collect a variety of fiction and non-fiction pieces of writing to show a good range of your child's abilities.

RESULTS

On results day, your child will not receive a grade or level as students do for their GCSEs or A levels. Instead, they will be given a scaled score for each subject. It is scaled so that there is no difference from year to year. If your child's score is 100 or higher, they are thought to be working at the expected standard for their age. If their score is 99 or lower, they are thought to be working below the expected standard.

Assessment guidance

At the end of Year 6, your student will sit three papers as part of the Key Stage 2 English national curriculum tests. Below you will find a summary of what to expect. You can find full details about all of the papers in the English reading test framework and the English grammar, spelling and punctuation framework on the government's website.

Grammar, punctuation and spelling

Paper 1: questions
Students will have 45 minutes to complete all 49 questions. This paper is worth 50 marks in total and is made up of two types of question: multiple-choice answers and short answers. For multiple-choice questions, your student will have to give a 'non-verbal' response: tick a box, underline or circle an answer, for example. For short answer questions, they will have to give a short response: complete a sentence, replace an incorrect word, or give a short definition or explanation of a grammatical feature.

Paper 2: spelling
The spelling component of the test is administered by the classroom teacher. The teacher will read out 20 spellings using a script. For example, if the word to be spelled was 'according', the teacher would say: "One. The word is according. According to my mum, I should eat more vegetables. The word is according." The student must then write down the word, and will get a mark for every one they have spelled correctly. The test will take around 15 minutes, but it is not strictly timed.

Reading

In the reading test, students will be given a selection of around three or four texts in a short reading booklet. Students will have one hour to read the texts and answer the questions in the answer booklet. This paper is worth 50 marks in total. Your student will encounter four types of question:

- *Short answers* – one line or a box denotes that your student need only write several words, and sometimes just one word.
- *Several line answers* – several lines means that your student should write a longer response, up to two sentences.
- *Longer answers* – a box containing lines requires a longer, more structured response. Such answers usually involve giving an opinion and explaining your answer with evidence. P-E-E (point, evidence, explain) will be useful for longer answers.
- *Selected answers* – like the multiple-choice answers on the Grammar, punctuation and spelling paper, your student won't need to write any words for these questions.

Cognitive domain

In the accompanying Tutor Delivery Pack, the content domain for the Year 6 tests is explained. It details the topics that may be covered in the test, whereas the cognitive domain explains the cognitive processes required to respond to a question.

Reading
There are five strands to the reading cognitive domain and each domain has four levels from 1 (low) to 4 (high). The summary in italics is taken directly from the framework. The strands are:

- **A: accessibility of the target information** – *Where can the information be found?*
  Lower demand questions will clearly present the small amount of information students need to answer the question. Students will either be directed to the information or it will be reproduced along with the question. Higher demand questions will require students to draw together information from the text, which is not signposted by the question. There may also be a large amount of 'red herrings' in the text to act as distractors.

Assessment Guidance

- **B: complexity of the target information** – *What is the language of the text like?*
  Complexity is measured in three ways: lexico-grammatical density (the volume of complicated, unfamiliar words); concreteness / abstractness and familiarity of the information (how closely worded the question is to the target information). Lower demand questions will require the use of information with a low level of lexico-grammatical density, and whose ideas will be fairly concrete and worded similarly to the information required to form an answer. Conversely, higher demand questions will encourage abstract responses, will be more lexico-grammatically dense and will be worded differently from the source text.

- **C: task-specific complexity** – *How much work is needed to answer the question?*
  At a lower level, students will need to be able to retrieve information from the source texts. At a higher level, they may be required to make inferences and articulate abstract ideas.

- **D: response strategy** – *How easy is it to organise and present the answer?*
  At a lower level, students will need to write a few words or provide a non-verbal response. For higher-level questions, students will have to write extended answers and organise their thoughts appropriately.

- **E: technical knowledge required** – *How complex is the language of the question and / or the knowledge needed to answer it?* Questions on the lower end of the scale will not require understanding of complex words or technical language. At the higher end, knowledge of complex and technical vocabulary will be required.

Grammar, punctuation and spelling
There are four strands to the grammar, punctuation and spelling domain. They each have three levels, except for the response strategy strand, which has four. Refer to the framework for example questions at each level.

- **Cognitive level**
  At the lowest level, students will be expected to recall facts, and be able to identify linguistic features and understand their functions. Mid-range questions require some application of this knowledge to a given context. At the highest level, students will have to give an explanation of some kind: generally they will make a comparison or describe the effect of using a particular feature.

- **Response strategy**
  The response strategy is dictated by the question type. At the lower end of the scale, selected responses require the student to identify the correct answer from a series of choices. At the higher end, students are expected to construct an extended response without a given structure.

- **Abstraction rating**
  At the lowest level, the language used and context given will be familiar to the student – it may refer to school life or public transport, for example – whereas at the highest level, students will face words and context that are far more complex and infrequently encountered by children of their age.

- **Strategy support rating**
  Lower-level questions will provide plenty of support to help the student work out what they must do, such as modelling an example answer, whereas higher-level questions require the student to work out what the question is asking them to do and how they will formulate their answer.

Results

Previously, when students received their results from the Year 6 SATs papers, they were given a level between 2 and 6. This is no longer the case, as students are now given a scaled score for each subject: maths; reading; writing and grammar, punctuation and spelling. If the score is 100 or higher, the student is deemed to be working at the 'expected standard'. The score is scaled so that there is no differentiation in results from year to year, regardless of the perceived difficulty of any paper.

PROGRESS TRACKING

The progress tracker below will help you to record and recall your student's scores and performances as you work through this pack. As you may wish to use a test more than once (at the start and end of teaching a subject area, for example), there is space for you to record two scores for each test. There is also space for you to make notes on areas for further study.

	FIRST TRY	SECOND TRY	AREAS TO WORK ON
CHECKPOINT CHALLENGES			
Reading	/40	/40	
Writing			
Grammar and punctuation	/40	/40	
Spelling	/40	/40	
TOPIC TESTS			
1 Diagnostic lesson	/10	/10	
2 Question types	/10	/10	
3 Non-fiction features	/10	/10	
4 Finding answers	/10	/10	
5 Character, theme and language	/10	/10	
6 Meaning	/10	/10	
7 Making comparisons	/10	/10	
8 Poetry (similes and metaphors)	/10	/10	
9 Poetry (other figurative language)	/10	/10	
10 Audience and purpose	/10	/10	
11 The writing process	/10	/10	
12 The editing process	/10	/10	
13 Writing: articles	/10	/10	
14 Writing: explanations	/10	/10	
15 Writing: persuasive letters	/10	/10	
16 Writing: balanced arguments	/10	/10	
17 Writing fiction	/10	/10	
18 Nouns	/10	/10	
19 Pronouns and determiners	/10	/10	

PROGRESS TRACKING

	FIRST TRY	SECOND TRY	AREAS TO WORK ON
20 Adjectives and adverbs	/10	/10	
21 Verbs – present	/10	/10	
22 Verbs – past	/10	/10	
23 Verbs – future and modal	/10	/10	
24 Conjunctions and prepositions	/10	/10	
25 Sentence types	/10	/10	
26 Subject and object	/10	/10	
27 Clauses	/10	/10	
28 Standard English	/10	/10	
29 Basic sentence punctuation	/10	/10	
30 Commas	/10	/10	
31 Parenthesis	/10	/10	
32 Colons and semi-colons	/10	/10	
33 Apostrophes	/10	/10	
34 Punctuating speech	/10	/10	
35 Hyphens and single dashes	/10	/10	
36 Word families	/10	/10	
37 Synonyms, antonyms and homophones	/10	/10	
38 Tricky spellings	/10	/10	
PRACTICE PAPERS			
Reading	/50	/50	
GPS Paper 1: questions	/50	/50	
GPS Paper 2: spelling	/20	/20	

TALK ABOUT THE TEST

Look at the test you have recently taken. Fill in the boxes with help from your tutor.

The test I took was ... **My score was ...**
(Your tutor will fill this in.)

/

I felt ...
(Circle the face that best describes how you felt when you took the test.)

confident about the test.

unsure about the test.

really confused about the test.

Next time I do a test, I will ...
(What could you do differently? Did you rush through? Did you read the questions properly?)

The questions I found easiest were ...
(Which questions did you find easy?)

because ...
(Explain why you found these questions easy. Maybe you find tick box questions easy or prefer to explain your answer. Perhaps you have practised the topic a lot at school.)

TALK ABOUT THE TEST

The questions I found hardest were ...
(Which questions did you find tricky?)

because ...
(Explain why you found these questions tricky.)

To improve these areas, we are going to ...
(Here your tutor will explain how he/she is going to help you become confident in these areas.)

At home, we can ...
(Here your tutor will explain what you can do at home to become more confident in these areas.)

Checkpoint Challenges

How to use

Each of these checkpoint challenges is intended to cover one of the four main topic areas addressed in the national curriculum tests: spelling; grammar and punctuation; writing and reading.

Each challenge can be used in a number of ways:

- as a diagnostic test
- as a homework activity
- as a main activity if extra time is available
- as revision closer to the tests
- at the end of the relevant section of the lesson plans.

These challenges are designed to provide informal test practice, in addition to the more formal practice papers on pages 87–142.

Reading

The reading checkpoint challenge has 40 marks in total, and should take around one hour to complete. The following texts have been provided for the student to read:

- Poetry: *How the Tortoise Got Its Shell*; *It's Spring*
- Non-fiction text: *Living with Diabetes*
- Fiction text: *The Pomegranate Seeds*

The student will need to read each of the three texts on pages 14–16 and then answer the questions on pages 17–27. A mark scheme can be found on pages 143–145.

Writing

The writing checkpoint challenge contains four separate activities, intended to provide a variety of starting points for writing practice. These are:

- Task A: a brief for a short story
- Task B: a stimulus from which to continue writing a fiction piece
- Task C: a brief for a piece of persuasive writing
- Task D: a brief for a piece of explanatory writing.

The student can choose one or more of the writing tasks on pages 28–29, depending on how much time is available. They will need to be supplied with additional lined paper on which to write their responses. Please remember that there is no writing test at the end of Year 6. Instead, students' writing ability will be teacher-assessed. Because of this, you may wish to make use of the writing checkpoint challenges early in the year.

Grammar and punctuation

The grammar and punctuation checkpoint challenge has 40 marks in total, and should take around 45 minutes to complete. All questions on pages 30–43 should be answered, and a mark scheme can be found on pages 149–152.

Spelling

The spelling checkpoint challenge has 40 marks in total, and should take around one hour to complete. This challenge is designed to provide a variety of spelling-based questions and activities. All questions on pages 44–48 should be answered, and a mark scheme can be found on pages 153–154.

READING CHECKPOINT CHALLENGE (POETRY)

How the Tortoise Got Its Shell

Come to my feast!
cried the great god Zeus.
Today I shall be wed!
And from each corner of the earth
all Zeus's creatures sped...

The fliers and the creepers,
the long, the short, the tall;
the crawlers and the leapers,
the feathered, furred, and bald;
hunters, biters, finders, fighters,
hooters, whistlers, roarers;
squeakers, screamers, squawkers, dreamers,
nibblers, gulpers, borers.
Paws and claws from the hills and shores
from south, from north, from west and east,
from mountain tops and forest floors
all Zeus's creatures joined the feast
except
the tortoise.

They raved, they pranced, they feasted, danced;
six days and nights each creature stayed
to chatter, flatter, clap and cheer
at the great god Zeus's grand parade
except
the tortoise.

Next day . . .
Why weren't you there, my friend, asked Zeus,
the day that I was wed?

The tortoise smiled her small, slow smile
and raised her small, slow head.

A wedding feast is fun, I guess,
but I'm a simple one.
I'm happy by myself, she said.
There's no place quite like home!

How dare you stay away! roared Zeus.
I'll show you just what for!
From this day on you'll carry your home
on your back, for evermore!

Judith Nicholls

It's Spring

It's spring
And the garden is changing its clothes,
Putting away
Its dark winter suits,
Its dull scarves
And drab brown overcoats.

Now, it wraps itself in green shoots,
Slips on blouses
Sleeved with pink and white blossom,
Pulls on skirts of daffodil and primrose,
Snowdrop socks and purple crocus shoes,
Then dances in the sunlight.

John Foster

READING CHECKPOINT CHALLENGE (NON-FICTION TEXT)

Living with diabetes

What is diabetes?
Diabetes develops when your pancreas (an organ in your body) stops working properly. Your blood contains a type of sugar called glucose, which is used by your cells for energy. Normally, the pancreas helps to make sure you have the correct amount of glucose in your blood. It does this by producing a hormone called insulin that allows glucose into your cells.
With diabetes, the pancreas does not make insulin and you may end up with too much glucose in your blood and not enough in your cells, making you more and more tired and thirsty.

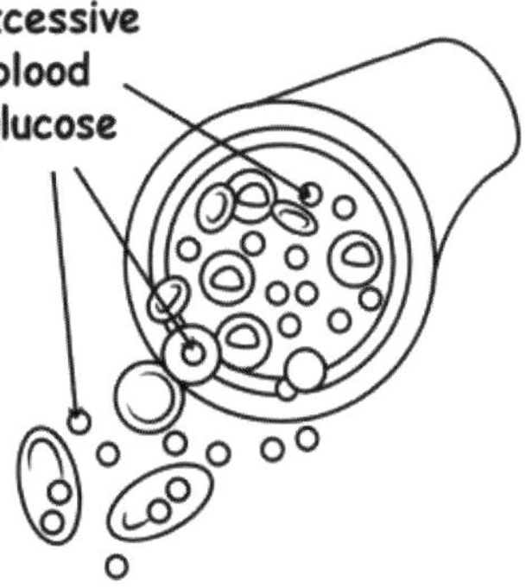

Insulin injections
If you have diabetes, you may need to inject insulin into your body to feel better. You may need two injections per day: one before breakfast and one before your evening meal. Many people use a pen injector, which has a small needle. People say it feels no worse than a pin prick. Even so, it is important to inject yourself in a different place every time.

Blood sugar level
If you have to inject insulin, you also have to make sure you have enough glucose in your blood. The best way to do this is to eat a healthy diet that releases glucose steadily throughout each day. This means eating a mix of carbohydrates (for example, pasta, potatoes and rice); fresh fruit and vegetables; protein (for example, meat, fish and eggs); and dairy products (for example, milk and cheese). It also means usually avoiding very sugary foods such as sweets and fizzy drinks. People with diabetes often eat something at bedtime to make sure they have enough glucose in their blood to last through the night.

You must also test how much sugar is in your system at least once a day by doing a blood test. First, you prick your finger with a device called a lancet. You then squeeze out a drop of blood onto a test strip and put it into a blood glucose meter, which gives you a reading. A reading between 4 and 7 is the target.

Hypoglycaemia
Sometimes, if you haven't eaten enough or at regular intervals, your blood glucose level may drop making you feel ill. This is known as having a 'hypo' (or hypoglycaemia attack). You might feel sick, shaky, sweaty or cold. You might become irritated, confused or anxious. In this situation, it is important to eat sugary foods as your body needs glucose quickly! You should eat some chocolate or biscuits or have a fizzy drink (not a diet one) for a quick glucose boost. Once you feel a bit better, you should also eat something healthy like some cereal or a sandwich.

Famous diabetics
Exercise is important if you are diabetic because it helps keep you healthy and prevents you putting on weight. Providing you can control your glucose level, you could even become an elite athlete. Famous diabetic sportspeople include: Henry Slade, the England rugby player; Steve Redgrave, the Olympic rower; and Scott Allan, the Scottish professional footballer.

Using a lancet to test blood sugar levels

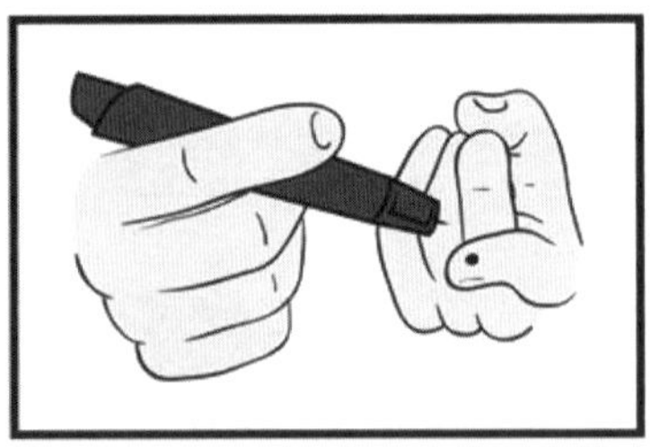

READING CHECKPOINT CHALLENGE (FICTION TEXT)

The Pomegranate Seeds

In Ancient Greece, Demeter, the goddess of the earth, looked after the harvest. She had a daughter called Persephone. Of all the spirits, Persephone was the most beautiful. Flowers would open proudly and trees would bow gracefully to show their love for her. Demeter's heart swelled with pride and the farmers' crops would grow tall and healthy.

Far below, in the caverns of the Underworld, there was no light or happiness or hope. The spectres that haunted the cold darkness knew nothing of the brightness above. Only Hades, their king, knew what they were missing. He remembered the bounty of life, colour and beauty overhead. Despite his own power and riches, he was bitter with envy for his brother Zeus, the ruler of the upper world. One day, when his bitterness grew too great, Hades harnessed his horses to his black chariot and galloped out into the world above. His dark, billowing cloak blotted out the sun. His horses' eyes glowed as red as hot coals and the air hissed dangerously like a thousand cats. Hades flew over a meadow, where his gaze fell upon Persephone playing with the nymphs. Her beauty warmed his cold veins and sweetened his sour heart. Here at last, he thought, was a queen to fill the Underworld with light and hope.

In the meadow, the sun suddenly disappeared. The nymphs looked up in horror at the ghastly dark shadow hovering over them. A sudden chill pricked their skin like icy needles and then it was gone. The sun shone hotly again and the stream gurgled merrily. The nymphs looked around for Persephone and screamed. Where she had lain, the grass was flat and frozen.

Hades drove his chariot into the darkest depths of the Underworld and locked Persephone up. He bought her delicious food, but she refused to eat. A week went by and finally, in desperation, Persephone ate six pomegranate seeds and wept.

She was not the only one. In the upper world, Demeter was filled with despair. She forgot all about the flowers and plants and her interest in the harvest. Crops withered and rotted as the soil became infertile. The people prayed to her but their pleas fell upon ears deafened by sorrow. Famine gnawed at their stomachs and their strength. The people turned to Zeus himself, begging him for help in great waves of pitiful prayers.

Zeus considered what to do. He had seen his brother snatch Persephone and imprison her. He summoned Demeter and told her: "It is the law of the Gods that if a living soul eats in the Underworld, then they must stay with the dead forever. Persephone has eaten food: six pomegranate seeds. But I have also seen the suffering that infects both the upper world and the world of Hades. This I command: for each seed eaten, Persephone must stay one month in the Underworld with Hades. For the remaining months, she is free to live in the upper world amongst the mortals and with you."

So, for six months each year, the world waits, cold and bare, for Persephone's return from the darkness. At last, she emerges and life blossoms and blooms across the land. Six months later, after the harvest, she must return to the land of shadows and the long, dark wait for her to reappear begins again.

Reading Checkpoint Challenge

Read the poem *It's Spring* and answer the following questions.

1. Find and copy the first example of personification used by the poet.

....

....

1 mark

2. Which three alliterative adjectives does the poet use to describe the appearance of winter?

....

1 mark

3. The poet uses personification in the second verse to describe what is happening in the garden. Give two examples of things the garden is 'doing'?

1) ....

2) ....

1 mark

4. How do you think the poet feels about winter and spring? Use evidence from the text to support your answer.

....

....

....

2 marks

READING CHECKPOINT CHALLENGE

Read the poem *How the Tortoise Got Its Shell* and answer the following questions.

5. This poem is an example of one of the following genres. Which one is it? Tick one.

- ☐ an explanation
- ☐ a fable
- ☐ a report
- ☐ a diary

1 mark

6. Explain why the poet has used italics in the following lines from the poem.

Come to my feast!
cried the great god Zeus.
Today I shall be wed!

....

....

1 mark

7. The poet doesn't name any animals, except the tortoise. Draw lines to match the words from the poem to the creatures they are likely to be.

fliers
crawlers
borers
hooters
roarers
gulpers

moles
seagulls
lions
frogs
centipedes
owls

1 mark

READING CHECKPOINT CHALLENGE

8. Find and copy an example of alliteration the poet uses to describe the tortoise.

....

....

....

1 mark

9. The tortoise's shell is its home.

What do you call this type of comparison? Tick one.

- ☐ simile
- ☐ onomatopoeia
- ☐ personification
- ☐ metaphor

1 mark

READING CHECKPOINT CHALLENGE

Read the non-fiction text *Living with Diabetes* and answer the following questions.

10. In which organ in the body is insulin produced?

....

1 mark

11. Draw lines to match the technical words from the text to their meanings.

word
insulin
glucose
hypoglycaemia
diabetic
carbohydrate

meaning
someone with diabetes
illness brought on by low blood glucose
a hormone that allows glucose into cells
a type of food that contains sugars and starches
a type of sugar

1 mark

12. How can someone with diabetes remain healthy? Give two suggestions.

1) ....

2) ....

1 mark

13. Why should you not give a diet fizzy drink to someone experiencing a hypoglycaemia attack? Use evidence from the text to support your answer.

....

....

1 mark

READING CHECKPOINT CHALLENGE

14. Complete the table by putting the following foods into the correct categories:

cheese broccoli rice salmon
yoghurt peach bread chicken breast

carbohydrates	fruit and vegetables
protein	**dairy products**

1 mark

15. Complete this sentence:

It is important that a diabetic eats at bedtime because ...

....

....

1 mark

16. Find and copy the parenthesis in the first sentence of the article's first paragraph.

....

1 mark

17. What are the three pieces of equipment you need to do a blood glucose test?

1) ....

2) ....

3) ....

1 mark

Reading Checkpoint Challenge

18. Using information from the text, tick one box in each row to show whether each statement is a fact or an opinion.

	fact	opinion
The hormone insulin helps your body use glucose for energy.		
An insulin injection feels no worse than a pin prick.		
Anyone with diabetes can become an elite athlete.		
A blood glucose level below 4 might indicate hypoglycaemia.		

1 mark

19. When injecting insulin, why do you think it is important to inject yourself in a different place every time?

....

....

1 mark

20. Complete the table with the symptoms of having a 'hypo'.

emotional symptoms	physical symptoms

1 mark

READING CHECKPOINT CHALLENGE

21. a) Why it is important for a diabetic to inject insulin *before* a meal?
Use evidence from the text to support your answer.

....

....

....

....

2 marks

b) Explain why a diabetic *should not* take their insulin a long time before a meal.
Use evidence from the text to support your answer.

....

....

....

....

2 marks

READING CHECKPOINT CHALLENGE

Read the fiction text *The Pomegranate Seeds* and answer the following questions.

22. In what order do the events of the story take place? Complete the table with numbers 1-6.

event	order
Hades spots Persephone in a field.	
Persephone eats the pomegranate seeds.	
The crops fail.	
Persephone is imprisoned.	
Hades leaves the underworld.	
Zeus summons Demeter.	

1 mark

23. a) What is a synonym of the word *spectre* in the second paragraph?

....

1 mark

b) Read this sentence from the story:

He remembered the bounty of life, colour and beauty overhead.

In this sentence, which of the words below is *bounty* closest in meaning to? Tick one.

- ☐ plenty
- ☐ treasure
- ☐ magic
- ☐ beauty

2 marks

READING CHECKPOINT CHALLENGE

24. Find and copy two similes from the second paragraph.

1) ....

2) ....

1 mark

25. What mistake does Persephone make that means she must stay in the Underworld?
Use evidence from the text to support your answer.

....

1 mark

26. Find and copy two noun phases that describe Hades.

1) ....

2) ....

1 mark

27. Read this sentence from the story:
Her beauty warmed his cold veins and sweetened his sour heart.

Which of the grammar terms below does the author use in this sentence?

☐ synonyms ☐ noun phrases ☐ antonyms

1 mark

28. Read this sentence from the story:
She was not the only one.

Which other character was weeping?

....

1 mark

READING CHECKPOINT CHALLENGE

29. Explain how Demeter's mood affects the crops. Use evidence from the text to support your answer.

....

....

....

....

1 marks

30. The character of Zeus appears in *The Pomegranate Seeds* and the poem *How the Tortoise Got Its Shell*. Explain how the character of Zeus is presented differently in each text. Use evidence from the text to support your answer.

....

....

....

....

....

2 marks

READING CHECKPOINT CHALLENGE

31. *The Pomegranate Seeds* and *How the Tortoise Got Its Shell* both explain how something came to exist in the world. What does *The Pomegranate Seeds* explain the existence of? Use evidence from the text to support your answer.

....

....

....

....

2 marks

32. Rewrite the title of *The Pomegranate Seeds* in the same style as *How the Tortoise Got Its Shell* to show your understanding of the story.

....

....

1 mark

Writing Checkpoint Challenge

Task A: Write a short story

A fable is a short story that often features magical animals that can speak. It ends with a moral (a lesson). Your task is to write a fable. The title is *The Three Curious Cats*. You will need to decide:

- who is in the fable
- what the cats are curious about
- what happens to the cats
- what lesson the reader might take from the fable.

Remember to think about the way traditional tales and fables are written, including how they start and how they end. Try to include some action, speech and description.

Task B: Continue a piece of fiction (diary)

Read the diary entry below.

Friday 26 August

What a meal! Well, it turns out Mum and Dad had been keeping a big secret. I've begged them so many times to take me there. And now we've been! I was in awe standing outside the famous polished bronze doors of 'Ambrosia', the world's number one restaurant. A tall, smiling waiter opened the doors for us and showed us to our table. Mum told me I could choose anything (anything!) because it was my birthday.

Your task is to continue this diary entry on a separate sheet of paper by describing the meal you ate that evening. Be as imaginative as you like and think about:

- what you chose to eat
- how you would describe it to someone
- how the food looked, tasted and smelled.

Remember to include the features and devices of both fiction and diary writing. Your purpose is to entertain an audience. Try to include effective adjectives and use interesting words and phrases to make your writing flow.

Writing Checkpoint Challenge

Task C: Write a persuasive text

Read the comment by a reader called *buzzoffbees* posted on an online article about garden insects.

buzzoffbees 3 minutes ago
My life is being ruined by bees in my garden. They are everywhere, buzzing angrily. I'm sure my sunflowers are drooping because the bees are clambering all over them. When I go into the garden, it's so frightening: bees circle around my head looking for somewhere to sting. I don't let my children out anymore! One huge bee even got into the kitchen; I've kept the windows shut ever since! They're such pests.

Use the facts below to write an informal reply to *buzzoffbees* to persuade them that they are wrong about bees. Remember to:

- use the facts in the factsheet below
- use emotive language
- be persuasive
- use connectives to link your ideas.

The benefits of bees
Bees don't just provide honey: they live together in a complex society. Bees only sting when disturbed or attacked and the male drone bees don't even have stingers. Bees pollinate lots of plants in our gardens and most of the fruit and vegetables we eat. It would cost £1.8 billion a year for farmers to pollinate their own crops. Bees are under threat because of disappearing habitat, pollution and climate change.

Task D: Write an explanation

You have invented a special hat. You want a big company to make and sell it so you can become a millionaire. Your task is to write an explanation of:

- what your hat does and what makes it special
- how it works.

Be imaginative but don't forget to use technical vocabulary, formal language, conjunctions and the present tense to provide a detailed explanation.

GRAMMAR AND PUNCTUATION CHECKPOINT CHALLENGE

1. What is the name for a word that replaces a noun or noun phrase?

....

1 mark

2. Circle the words in the cloud below that should have a capital letter.

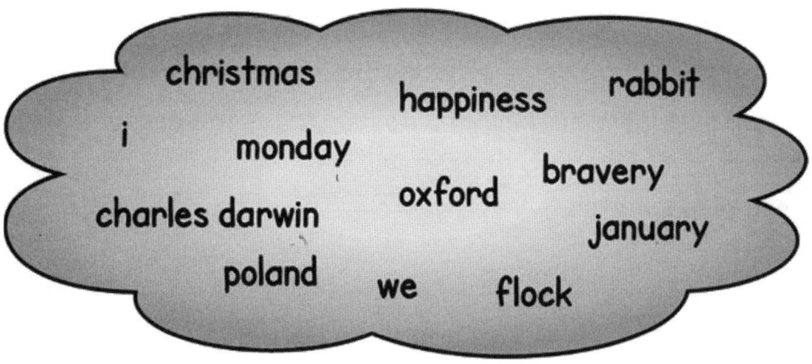

2 marks

3. a) Which of these sentences is the odd one out? Tick one.

- ☐ I'm so annoyed we missed the ferry, aren't you?
- ☐ What a shame we didn't arrive on time!
- ☐ What time is the next ferry?
- ☐ Are we going to get a place on the next ferry?

1 mark

b) Why it is the odd one out?

....

1 mark

4. Read the sentence below, then add in the missing inverted commas in the correct place. You do not need to add any other punctuation.

I've got a great idea, I said. It's too hot, isn't it? Let's stop and get some ice-cream.

1 mark

GRAMMAR AND PUNCTUATION CHECKPOINT CHALLENGE

5. Rewrite the sentences below using the contracted form of the underlined words. Remember to punctuate your answer correctly.

You should have kept that a secret.

They will not be happy until it is all mended properly.

You are late and they are disappointed.

1 mark

6. There are five past tense verbs hidden in this word search (the words run across only). Circle them and then copy them out in alphabetical order. Remember you are only looking for verbs in the simple past tense.

e	z	b	d	t	h	r	o	w	e
c	v	y	q	b	e	g	a	n	i
k	u	b	w	o	n	h	p	h	y
m	r	a	n	r	z	x	z	j	r
a	d	f	t	h	k	n	o	o	h
c	w	i	j	a	s	a	i	d	u
q	b	k	f	t	h	r	e	w	g
u	b	e	g	i	n	m	v	b	i
r	x	g	n	k	w	r	w	k	z
e	l	p	m	b	u	w	w	u	v

1 mark

7. Circle all the adjectives in the sentence below.

My younger sister is quick and nimble but your older brother is very strong.

1 mark

GRAMMAR AND PUNCTUATION CHECKPOINT CHALLENGE

8. Add the correct punctuation to the end of each of the sentences below.

Couldn't we all stop arguing and try to get along

How delicious that milkshake was

I read a comic every morning; I draw my own cartoons in the evening

1 mark

9. Rewrite the sentences below in the passive voice.

A cricket ball shattered the living room window.

....

The enormous, noisy lorry ran over the little girl's doll.

....

1 mark

10. Here's an advert for a new ice-lolly.

a) Find and circle all of the modal verbs in the advert.

b) Use them to complete the puzzle below to reveal the name of the new product.

c) What is the name of the ice-lolly?

....

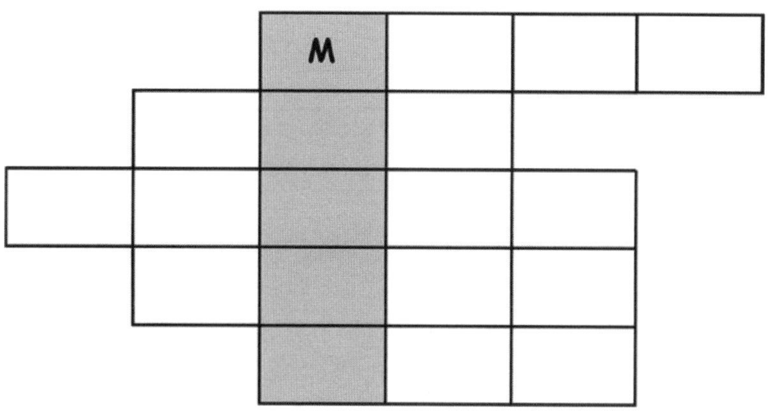

1 mark

GRAMMAR AND PUNCTUATION CHECKPOINT CHALLENGE

11. Draw lines to match the adjectives to the adverbs. Be careful, one pair is a trick (don't join those words up!).

moody	angrily
simple	moodily
angry	well
good	fast
hard	hardly
fast	simply

1 mark

12. Rewrite the sentences below by moving the commas to the correct places.

Harriet, ate a slice of pizza two cartons of apple, juice an orange and a boiled egg for lunch.

....

....

....

1 mark

Bravery generosity calmness under pressure and reliability, are some, of his characteristics.

....

....

....

1 mark

GRAMMAR AND PUNCTUATION CHECKPOINT CHALLENGE

13. The letters in the twelve prepositions below have been muddled up. Unscramble them and complete the table. Two have been done for you.

~~trefa~~ earn incse ovre unlit ta
~~theabna~~ roughth avobe oga ruding racoss

prepositions showing time	prepositions showing position
after	beneath

1 mark

14. Which set of possessive pronouns best completes the sentence below? Tick one option.

Please do ....chores: the dog needs ....tea and the rabbits need ....hutch cleaning out.

☐ yours, its, theirs
☐ my, his, its
☐ your, its, their
☐ your, it's, their

1 mark

15. Add a pair of brackets to the correct place in the sentence below.

I was surprised that I enjoyed the white-water rafting I usually avoided terrifying activities.

1 mark

GRAMMAR AND PUNCTUATION CHECKPOINT CHALLENGE

16. a) Draw lines to match the correct subordinate clause to its main clause.

main clause
My dad always wears a thick jumper
Our dog Pip would bark madly
I sometimes cheat at cards

subordinate clause
although I would never admit it.
even when it is baking hot.
whenever someone knocked at the door.

b) Rewrite each sentence, putting the subordinate clause first. Make sure you use the correct punctuation.

....

....

....

1 mark

17. Circle all the determiners in the passage below.

Some people are tall. Other people are short. The tallest person ever measured 8 feet 11 inches. Nowadays, a man from Holland is on average 6 feet tall.

1 mark

18. Insert a colon in the correct place in each of the sentences below.

In an emergency, do the following exit your room, avoid using the lift and raise the alarm.

Our journey just got worse and worse the car broke down in the rain.

1 mark

GRAMMAR AND PUNCTUATION CHECKPOINT CHALLENGE

19. There are four verbs in the present perfect form in the passage below. The first one is *has taken*. Find the remaining three and copy them on to the lines below.

The cold weather <u>has taken</u> over completely. The blast of air from the north has frozen the lake. The winds were vicious and have destroyed all the fishing nets. However, the crisp snow that sparkles in the sunlight has captivated everyone.

....

3 marks

20. Rewrite each of the phrases below using an apostrophe to show possession.

the chair belonging to the girl

....

the toys belonging to the children

....

the howling belonging to the wolves

....

the basketballs belonging to Thomas

....

1 mark

GRAMMAR AND PUNCTUATION CHECKPOINT CHALLENGE

21. a) Which of these sentences is the odd one out? Tick one.

- ☐ She runs very fast around the athletics track.
- ☐ I will never finish all my homework!
- ☐ The meeting starts at 10 o'clock tomorrow morning.
- ☐ Is it going to be sunny today?

b) Why is it the odd one out?

....

1 mark

22. Rewrite the sentences below changing the direct speech to reported speech.

"I still don't know how to ride a bike," admitted Tyler.

....

....

My mum asked, "Have you remembered your PE kit?"

....

....

1 mark

GRAMMAR AND PUNCTUATION CHECKPOINT CHALLENGE

23. Draw lines to match the non-Standard English to the correct Standard English.

non-Standard English
barking
cheesed off
geezer
jammy
minted
scarper

Standard English
annoyed
crazy
wealthy
run away
man
lucky

1 mark

24. Extra information can be added to a sentence in a parenthesis. Which of these punctuation marks can you use to separate a parenthesis from the rest of the sentence? Tick three.

☐ a pair of brackets

☐ a pair of question marks

☐ a pair of colons

☐ a pair of dashes

☐ a pair of commas

☐ a pair of hyphens

1 mark

25. Underline the relative clause in each of the sentences below.

My great uncle, who fought in the Korean War, celebrated his 90th birthday recently.

We are proud of our new cows, which came from a farm in Devon.

Sir Gwyn Broadsword, whose arms were short and whose hands were tiny, didn't enjoy fighting.

1 mark

GRAMMAR AND PUNCTUATION CHECKPOINT CHALLENGE

26. Rewrite the sentences below, adding hyphens where they are needed.

The ex footballer bought a sports car at an eye watering price.

....

....

My sister in law likes to re cover her armchairs with old fashioned materials.

....

....

1 mark

27. Circle all the conjunctions in the passage below.

Your body is made up of organs. Your skin is an organ. It is waterproof and stretchy. If you step forward, you use about 200 muscles under your skin. Muscles can only pull so they work in pairs. When you cut yourself, your skin forms a scab. It might look nasty but it stops germs getting in.

1 mark

28. For each sentence below, tick the correct box to show where the semi-colon should go.

Bex loves to watch ↑ old movies ↑ her friends prefer ↑ reality TV shows.

☐ ☐ ☐

Camels are suited to life ↑ in the desert ↑ they can go for ↑ days without water.

☐ ☐ ☐

1 mark

GRAMMAR AND PUNCTUATION CHECKPOINT CHALLENGE

29. Underline the subject and circle the object in each of the sentences below.

Early every morning, the milkman delivers his dairy products to our street.

The author was delighted by the latest reviews of his new book.

A stooping man, who was wearing a long coat, approached the tall gates with uncertainty.

1 mark

30. Find and copy one noun phrase from each sentence in question 29 that you haven't already underlined or circled.

....

....

....

1 mark

31. Find three adverbials in the sentence below and write them in the correct place in the table.

At the crack of dawn, a team of policeman arrived by helicopter at the crime scene.

how?	where?	when?

1 mark

GRAMMAR AND PUNCTUATION CHECKPOINT CHALLENGE

32. Rewrite the sentences below to make them into questions. Remember to punctuate your answers correctly.

You did not know that we are going to Disneyland tomorrow.

....

You and Dad decided when to go shopping.

....

1 mark

33. In what order would you put the following elements in a formal letter? Complete the table with numbers 1–6 in the order they should appear.

formal letter elements	order
your own address and the date	
Yours sincerely,	
your signature	
the reason you are writing	
the name and address of the person you are writing to	
Dear Sir/Madam,	

1 mark

34. Rewrite the sentences below to make the subjects and the verbs agree.

Has you done the mowing yet? It look as if it are about to rain.

....

....

Please writes to your grandma. You doesn't want to hurt her feelings, does you?

....

....

1 mark

GRAMMAR AND PUNCTUATION CHECKPOINT CHALLENGE

35. Tick two boxes in each sentence to show where the commas should go.

Whenever Georgie ☐ felt sad ☐ she went to visit her aunt ☐ uncle ☐ and their tortoise Gerald.

Although Max's room ☐ was smelly ☐ untidy ☐ and dusty ☐ he thought it was just perfect.

Even ☐ if I agreed ☐ to watch you do it ☐ I won't join in with the singing ☐ dancing or acting.

1 mark

36. The verbs in the following sentence are all in the same tense. Which tense is it? Tick one.

The sun was shining, the waves were lapping on the shore and the crabs were scuttling on the sand.

- ☐ simple past
- ☐ past progressive
- ☐ past perfect
- ☐ present progressive

1 mark

37. Tick one box in each row to show if the sentences need hyphens or a single dash at the places indicated.

sentence	hyphen	single dash
Usain Bolt is a lightning ? quick runner.		
I can sing like Adele ? at least, my mum says so!		
Its razor ? sharp teeth and needle ? like claws were petrifying.		

1 mark

GRAMMAR AND PUNCTUATION CHECKPOINT CHALLENGE

38. Underline the imperative verbs in the commands below.

If you see the warning light, stop immediately and call for help.

When the dough has doubled in size, remove it from the bowl and knock out the air.

1 mark

39. Circle all five expanded noun phrases in the passage below.

When I got home, I was surprised to discover a large, shaggy-haired dog sitting outside my front door. It looked up at me with its friendly, intelligent eyes and whined. I didn't know anyone with a dog so I took it inside and gave it some fresh water.

1 mark

40. a) Which of these sentences is the odd one out? Tick one.

☐ She has not visited Sheffield since 2012.

☐ I have printed out a copy of my story.

☐ They had eaten far too much pizza for lunch.

☐ I haven't told you my incredible news yet.

b) Explain why it is the odd one out.

....

....

1 mark

SPELLING CHECKPOINT CHALLENGE

1. Which of these words is spelled incorrectly? Tick one.

☐ immortal
☐ imperfect
☐ inpossible
☐ improbable

1 mark

2. Circle the two correct plural spellings below.

Horses partys journies roofs boyes

1 mark

3. Underline the two words that rhyme with each other.

rough though bought ploughed thought coughed

1 mark

4. Write the correct spelling of the words listed below.

agresive	temprature	guverment	fourty
....	....	....	....

2 marks

5. Choose the right set of words to complete the sentences below. Tick one.

It may be .... to.............................. .... to change the law.

☐ neccessary, persuade, parliment
☐ necessary, perswayed, parliament
☐ necessery, persuade, parliament
☐ necessary, persuade, parliament

1 mark

6. Write a homophone for each of the words below.

a) to → ....

c) peace → ....

b) here → ....

d) brake → ....

2 marks

SPELLING CHECKPOINT CHALLENGE

7. a) What is the root word found in all of the words below?

television revision envisage invisibility

....

1 mark

b) What is the meaning of this root word? Circle one.

the ability to hear the ability to understand the ability to see the ability to appear

1 mark

8. Complete this crossword. The ten answers are all nouns. The first letter of each has been completed for you.

<u>Across</u>
3. a dark mark on your skin caused by an injury
6. a sports person who is not paid
7. a place where people are buried
9. a person who lives next to you
10. a bright flash of light in a storm

<u>Down</u>
1. a person in the army
2. a line of people waiting their turn
4. the area between your neck and your arm
5. a place where you buy and eat a meal
8. a boat with a sail

5 marks

SPELLING CHECKPOINT CHALLENGE

9. a) All of the words below have missing silent letters. Spell them correctly to complete the puzzle below to reveal a hidden word. The first one has been done for you.

~~diffrent~~ ryme musle libary busness vegtable

d	i	f	f	e	r	e	n	t		

b) What is the hidden word?

....

3 marks

10. Draw lines to match each of the words below to its incorrectly spelled antonym. Write the correct spelling.

word
true
brave
lowest
quiet
enemy

antonym	correct spelling
lowd	
freind	
fallse	
heighest	
cowerdly	

2 marks

SPELLING CHECKPOINT CHALLENGE

11. Complete the table with the words listed below according to the suffixes they take. One has been done for you.

~~annoy~~ correspondent assist violent collect
obedient access clear reverse

+ ance	+ ence	+ ible
annoyance		

3 marks

12. Write a near homophone for each of the words below.

a) quiet → ....

c) effect → ....

b) accept → ....

d) advice → ....

2 marks

13. Add an appropriate prefix to each of the words below to give them a negative meaning.

a) happy → ....

c) lead → ....

b) flexible → ....

d) replaceable → ....

2 marks

14. Proofread the passage below. Underline the six incorrectly spelled words and write out the correct spellings below.

If you go to live in a forain country, it is a good idea to learn how to comyounicate in the main langwidge that is used there. It can be very orkwould not being able to make yourself understood; using a dicshunry really slows down conversations! Local people will really apreeshiate it if you give it a go.

....

....

3 marks

SPELLING CHECKPOINT CHALLENGE

15. Complete the phrases below with the plural spellings of these words:

inch potato half baby

ten ....

a bag full of ....

two ....

lots of crying ....

2 marks

16. Unscramble the letters in the middle column to find synonyms of the words in the first column. Write them in the synonym column.

word				synonym
miserable	→	hapnupy	→	
problem	→	tyfficuldi	→	
worried	→	srenvuo	→	
expensive	→	ceripy	→	
polite	→	cuortoeus	→	

4 marks

17. Tick the words that are spelled correctly.

☐ field
☐ cieling
☐ diesel
☐ seize
☐ decieve
☐ feirce

1 mark

18. Write the correct spelling of the words listed below.

fysical → ....

acheivement → ....

secretry → ....

embbarassed → ....

2 marks

19. Which of these words is spelled incorrectly? Tick one.

☐ suspicious
☐ ambicious
☐ ferocious
☐ delicious

1 mark

1 Diagnostic lesson (topic test)

1. Circle a number to show how confident you feel about the following areas of writing.

	low confidence				↔				high confidence	
Using capital letters and full stops	1	2	3	4	5	6	7	8	9	10
Using question marks and exclamation marks	1	2	3	4	5	6	7	8	9	10
Using inverted commas (speech marks)	1	2	3	4	5	6	7	8	9	10
Using commas in lists	1	2	3	4	5	6	7	8	9	10
Using apostrophes	1	2	3	4	5	6	7	8	9	10
Using colons and semi-colons	1	2	3	4	5	6	7	8	9	10
Using brackets, dashes and hyphens	1	2	3	4	5	6	7	8	9	10
Writing and linking main clauses	1	2	3	4	5	6	7	8	9	10
Writing and linking subordinate clauses	1	2	3	4	5	6	7	8	9	10
Writing and linking relative clauses	1	2	3	4	5	6	7	8	9	10
Using commas with clauses	1	2	3	4	5	6	7	8	9	10
Using different tenses	1	2	3	4	5	6	7	8	9	10
Using passive and modal verbs	1	2	3	4	5	6	7	8	9	10
Organising writing using paragraphs	1	2	3	4	5	6	7	8	9	10
Using conjunctions to link ideas	1	2	3	4	5	6	7	8	9	10
The speed of your handwriting	1	2	3	4	5	6	7	8	9	10
The look of your handwriting	1	2	3	4	5	6	7	8	9	10

2. List two things you enjoy about reading.

....

....

3. List two things about reading that you find difficult.

....

....

2 Question Types (Topic Test)

1. Underline the main clause in the sentences below. One has been done for you.

a) After the exams, <u>Hannah spent three weeks on holiday</u>.
b) Whenever I saw my grandma Alice, she always gave me a packet of sweets.

1 mark

2. Draw lines to match each sentence to the tense of the verb used.

I will never go jogging at night.	simple present
I would never go jogging at night.	future
I never go jogging at night.	modal

1 mark

3. Tick one option that best describes the underlined words in this sentence.

Monisha liked nothing better than <u>a huge plate of fish and chips</u>.

☐ alliteration ☐ expanded noun phrase
☐ metaphor ☐ fronted adverbial

1 mark

4. Add the correct punctuation to the sentence below.

It's a busy time of year ☐ most of our visitors arrive in August ☐

2 marks

5. Tick one box in each row to show whether each statement is true or false.

	true	false
A sentence always starts with a capital letter.		
A relative clause always comes at the start of a sentence.		
A phrase contains a noun and a verb.		
A command always ends with an exclamation mark.		

2 marks

6. Copy the three alliterative phrases from the sentence below.

Whenever I got home, friendly faces and sizzling sausages were always a warm welcome.

....

3 marks

3 Non-fiction features (topic test)

1. Circle the non-fiction text types in the cloud below.

encyclopaedia page
diary entry
science investigation
myth
adventure story
poem
product instructions
autobiography
play script
traditional tale

3 marks

2. Tick all the features you are likely to find in an explanation.

☐ a title starting with 'how'
☐ technical vocabulary
☐ the writer's opinion
☐ the writer's byline

1 mark

3. Tick all the features you are likely to find in a news article about a recent event.

☐ present tense
☐ different points of view
☐ an eye-catching headline
☐ chapters

1 mark

4. Tick all the features you are likely to find in a formal letter.

☐ Standard English
☐ a glossary
☐ the writer's address
☐ slang

1 mark

5. Draw lines to match the titles to the type of non-fiction text.
One has been done for you.

title
The Battle of Gettysburg (1863)
Should the police have guns?
How to make the most of your stay in Florida
Barry Snotter and the brilliant show!
Olympic Crisps, top of the podium every time

non-fiction text type
a theatre review
an information leaflet
a magazine advert
a historical report
a balanced argument

2 marks

6. List four features you could use to organise a balanced argument.

....

....

....

....

2 marks

4 Finding answers (topic test)

In 1970, Apollo 13 was approaching the Moon. On April 13th, an alarm flashed and the spacecraft shuddered. One of the fuel tanks had exploded and the spacecraft was losing power. Astronaut Jack Swigert radioed Mission Control and famously reported, "Houston, we've had a problem here." Apollo 13 was 300,000 miles away from home. The crew abandoned their Moon landing as the oxygen supply was beginning to fall. They entered the lunar module, fired the engine and set off back to Earth. It took two tense days, during which the crew used their ingenuity to filter the air as they worked in freezing conditions. Eventually, they re-entered the atmosphere and landed safely.

1. Find all the words in the text above that begin with *m* and copy them out below.

....

....

2 marks

2. Scan the text for the answers to the following questions.

a) What was the name of the spacecraft? ....

b) What date and year did the event take place? ....

c) Who radioed the bad news? ....

d) How far was the spacecraft from Earth? ....

e) What other name for Mission Control was used? ....

5 marks

3. Find and copy a word which means the same as *cleverness*.

....

1 mark

4. What caused the problem and what two effects did it have?

....

....

2 marks

5 CHARACTER, THEME AND LANGUAGE (TOPIC TEST)

1. Draw lines to match the terms below to the correct definitions.

term
character
theme
setting
plot

definition
the events that make up a story
where a story takes place
someone in a story; a person's personality and appearance
a pattern of ideas or a related sequence of events

2 marks

2. Read the sentences below and circle the most likely characteristic suggested about each character.

a) I've failed again, she thought. Mind you, I always do.

happy   optimistic   unconfident   cowardly

b) Mum had told me not to wake them up earlier than six, but I couldn't help it. It was my birthday after all and I wanted to make the most of it.

annoying   lazy   positive   wasteful

c) Stuart didn't enjoy playing tag in the playground: his shirt always ended up coming untucked from his trousers and his tie ended up slightly wonky.

careless   proud   carefree   smart

3 marks

3. Here are some sentences from a story. How would you describe the theme of the story?

Walking to school, Sunil spots a pound coin on the pavement.	He plays heads or tails with his sister and guesses correctly every time.
He wins the school raffle.	At lunchtime he finds a four-leaf clover.

The theme of the story is ....

1 mark

4. Complete the sentences below, adding words to create the mood indicated in brackets.

a) The wind ....through the trees. (calm)

b) Harris ....out of the room and slammed the door .... (angry)

c) "I can't wait to go!"................................ Vicki .... (excited)

d) The ...., ... door swung open................................. (mysterious)

4 marks

6 Meaning (topic test)

1. The sentences below include the same underlined word, but its meaning is different in each sentence. What does the word mean in each context? Circle one option in items a–d.

a) You might get a big fine if you keep dropping litter in the park.

a covered chair on poles | some rubbish | a group | absorbent material

b) My dog has just had a litter of beautiful puppies.

a covered chair on poles | some rubbish | a group | absorbent material

c) The cat's litter box needs clearing out; it smells terrible!

a covered chair on poles | some rubbish | a group | absorbent material

d) The rich merchant pulled back the curtains of the litter to see where he was.

a covered chair on poles | some rubbish | a group | absorbent material

4 marks

2. Circle the adjective in each sentence in question 1. Then write a synonym for each adjective on the answer lines below.

a) .... b) ....

c) .... d) ....

2 marks

3. What is the proper word for *reading between the lines*? Circle the correct word.

summarising | inferring | guessing

1 mark

4. What is a prediction?

....

1 mark

5. When you make a prediction about the next part of a story, which things are the most important to keep in mind? Tick two.

- ☐ to be imaginative
- ☐ the events so far
- ☐ the author's use of punctuation
- ☐ to end with a moral
- ☐ the names of the characters
- ☐ to make the bad guy 'badder'
- ☐ to make it funny
- ☐ the behaviour of the characters

2 marks

7 Making comparisons (topic test)

Read the following short passage:

The Speech

George stood up to speak. He didn't look up; not with all those eyes staring at him. His throat was dry and his head a little light. To his frustration, his hand was shaking, making the words on the paper hard to read. He opened his mouth. Nothing came out. He swallowed and now his legs felt wobbly. He almost yelped as a powerful hand gripped his shoulder and pushed down gently but firmly. His brother's smooth voice boomed in his ear, "Ladies and gentlemen, what my brother is trying to say is that it's an absolute pleasure to see you all here on this special occasion." George scowled down at the table. He could feel his cheeks burning. Under the table, he scrunched his speech into a ball as the audience laughed loudly at one of his brother's jokes.

1. Describe how the two brothers are different. You will need to make inferences (read between the lines) and use quotes from the text to support your answer.

....

....

....

4 marks

2. How do George's feelings change during the passage?

....

....

2 marks

3. What is a summary of a piece of writing? Tick two answers.

☐ the final paragraph

☐ a brief version of a plot

☐ a statement of the main message or idea

☐ the introduction

2 marks

4. Write a summary of the passage in one sentence.

....

....

2 marks

8 Poetry (Similes and Metaphors) (Topic Test)

1. Tick one box in each row to show if the phrase is a simile or a metaphor. One has been done for you.

phrase	simile	metaphor
It's as light as a feather.	✓	
I slept like a log.		
The sea was a mirror.		
She laughs like a hyena.		
My teacher is as wise as an owl.		
At sunset, the clouds were pink cotton wool.		
You are my sunshine.		

3 marks

2. Circle the two noun phrases that are being compared in each of the similes and metaphors below. One has been done for you.

a) My new friend is as cool as a cucumber.

b) The forest fire devoured the landscape like a beast from a fiery underworld.

c) The supporters of that politician are puppets on a string.

d) That invention of yours is as much use as a chocolate teapot.

2 marks

3. Complete the crossword.

<u>Across</u>
3. A tool used for cutting food
5. A device to protect you from the rain

<u>Down</u>
1. Words set to music and performed
2. A hot, dry, often sandy region
4. A large mammal with a hump and long neck

4. Now use the crossword answers to complete the similes and metaphors below.

a) I'm as thirsty as a .... in the ....

b) The tree was a wonderful, green ....

c) The wind in the trees was like a sad ....

d) The moon was a curved, silver ....

5 marks

9 POETRY (OTHER FIGURATIVE LANGUAGE) (TOPIC TEST)

1. Draw lines to match the term to the correct definition.

term
personification
alliteration
onomatopoeia

definition
a series of words beginning with the same letter
a word that copies the sound of the thing it is describing
a word that gives a non-human thing human characteristics

1 mark

2. Underline all of the alliterative words in the sentence below.
The cunning countess on the crimson couch counted her coins carefully.

1 mark

3. Underline the onomatopoeic words in the sentence below.
The thick, humid air cracked and rumbled with thunder.

1 mark

4. Underline the personification verb in the sentence below.
The flowers danced in the summer breeze.

1 mark

5. Complete each sentence with one of these words below.

sneaked rustled didn't

Then, write a letter in each box to show which type of figurative language each sentence uses.

P personification **A** alliteration **O** onomatopoeia

a) Overhead, the huge canopy of leaves .... in the wind. ☐

b) Dave's dog .... do walks. ☐

c) The sun .... behind a cloud. ☐

3 marks

6. Write one or more letters in each box to show which type of figurative language is used in each sentence. One has been done for you.

a) The waves tickled the sandy shore. **PA**

b) The wild wind blew the door closed with a bang. ☐

c) The smell of sizzling sausages dragged me into the kitchen. ☐

d) The fireworks screamed and popped. ☐

3 marks

10 AUDIENCE AND PURPOSE (TOPIC TEST)

1. What does the word *audience* mean when you are writing?

....

1 mark

2. What does the word *purpose* mean when you are writing?

....

1 mark

3. Draw lines to match the genre to its purpose. One has been done for you.

genre	purpose
an adventure novel	to persuade
a food advert	to entertain
a visitor's guide	to instruct
a bike maintenance manual	to inform

3 marks

4. Imagine you are writing a story book for five-year-old children. Name three ways you could make the writing suitable for your audience. One has been done for you.

......simple sentences.......... ....

2 marks

5. Read this short passage and decide who you think the audience is, and what you think is the purpose of the text. Give reasons for your answer.

Toddlers are very curious and love exploring. Keep your little angel safe in the kitchen by doing the following: fit safety catches on low cupboards and drawers; move your cleaning products to higher shelves; don't leave pot handles sticking out over the edge of the hob where little fingers can grab them; and dispose of plastic bags safely.

Audience: ....

Purpose: ....

Evidence: ....

....

3 marks

11 THE WRITING PROCESS (TOPIC TEST)

1. **Number these parts of the writing process from 1–5 in the order you should carry them out.**

☐ writing ☐ organising ☐ editing ☐ proofreading ☐ planning

1 mark

2. **a) When you are given a writing task, what is the first thing you should do? Tick one.**

☐ Write your ideas down quickly.
☐ Be clear on the audience and purpose.
☐ Organise your ideas.

b) What is the second thing? Tick one.

☐ Write your ideas down quickly.
☐ Be clear on the audience and purpose.
☐ Organise your ideas.

c) And the third thing? Tick one.

☐ Write your ideas down quickly.
☐ Be clear on the audience and purpose.
☐ Organise your ideas.

3 marks

3. **What is a paragraph and what is its purpose?**

....

....

2 marks

4. **What type of word can be used to link words, sentences and ideas?**

....

1 mark

5. **It is important to stay focused as you write. Below are some general tips to help. Complete them by writing 'Do' or 'Don't' in front of the following statements. One has been done for you.**

a) ......Don't...... write one long paragraph.

b) .... make it up as you go along.

c) ....follow your plan.

d) .... repeat the same points.

e) ....change genre halfway through.

f) .... link paragraphs using appropriate words and phrases.

g) .... give examples to support your points.

3 marks

12 THE EDITING PROCESS (TOPIC TEST)

1. The sentences below need developing. Rewrite them to improve how they sound. Think about the order of words, the choice of words and whether to use the active or passive voice.

a) Nick ate for breakfast bacon and eggs every day with toast and jam.

....

b) My boss is not an unkind person.

....

c) Reading and writing are enjoyed by Lauren.

....

3 marks

2. Write two questions you should ask yourself when checking your writing before proofreading. For example: ***Have I followed my plan?***

....?

....?

2 marks

3. The following passage contains ten spelling mistakes and punctuation errors. Find and underline them all, then rewrite the passage on a separate sheet of paper using the correct punctuation and spellings.

Putting on a suite of armour was a difficult task. It normally required the help of another person, First the knights squire helped the night into his padded tunic. This had peaces of chain mail sewn into it at the danger spots. It also had a number of laces; which were used to tie on piece's of armour. Once the armur was attached the last things to be put on were the gauntlets and helmet

5 marks

13 WRITING: ARTICLES (TOPIC TEST)

1. Name two places you might find a news article.

....

2 marks

2. Tick one option to complete the sentence.

In general, an article should ...

☐ give one person's point of view ☐ give both sides of a story.

1 mark

3. Tick one option to complete the sentence.

In general, an article contains ...

☐ facts ☐ opinions ☐ facts and opinions.

1 mark

4. Name four typical features of an article.

....

....

2 marks

5. Headlines are often short, snappy, eye-catching and alliterative.
Write a headline and a subheading for the stories below. One has been done for you.

Story A: Three blind mice ran after the farmer's wife, who cut off their tails with a carving knife. Did you ever see such a sight in your life as three blind mice?	**Headline:** Wife with knife attacks mice! **Subheading:** Mice recovering at vets 
Story B: Jack and Jill went up the hill to fetch a pail of water. Jack fell down and broke his crown and Jill came tumbling after.	**Headline:** .... **Subheading:** ....
Story C: Little Miss Muffet sat on a tuffet eating her curds and whey. Along came a spider and sat down beside her and frightened Miss Muffet away.	**Headline:** .... **Subheading:** ....

4 marks

14 WRITING: EXPLANATIONS (TOPIC TEST)

1. Which two words are often used to start an explanation? Circle two.

how   then   why   finally

1 mark

2. What is another way of saying *in chronological order*?

....

1 mark

3. Sort these conjunctions and linking phrases into the table below. One has been done for you.

~~later~~   so   next   therefore   as a result
finally   because   when   in this way   until

time links	causal links
later	

5 marks

4. In general, what tense do you write an explanation in? Tick one.

☐ past progressive   ☐ future
☐ simple past   ☐ simple present

1 mark

5. It is important to explain the meaning of technical words in an explanation. Complete the sentences below to explain each item to someone who has never seen or used them before.

A smartphone is ....

....

....

A games console is ....

....

....

2 marks

15 Writing: Persuasive Letters (Topic Test)

1. a) What should you write first in a formal letter?

....

b) Where should you write it on the page?

....

2 marks

2. Give two ways you could address the person you are writing to at the start of a letter.

a) ....

b) ....

2 marks

3. Explain what *Re:* means.

....

1 mark

4. Write the beginning of three *persuasive* sentences. One has been done for you.

1. It's very important that you ...

2. ....

3. ....

2 marks

5. What should you write in the last paragraph of a formal letter?

....

1 mark

6. When should you finish a formal letter with *Yours sincerely*? Tick one.

☐ when you want to be polite
☐ when you don't know the person
☐ when you know the person
☐ when you want to be friendly

1 mark

7. When should you finish a formal letter *Yours faithfully*? Tick one.

☐ when you want to be polite
☐ when you don't know the person
☐ when you know the person
☐ when you want to be friendly

1 mark

16 WRITING: BALANCED ARGUMENTS (TOPIC TEST)

1. In a balanced argument, what must you present?

....

1 mark

2. Number these parts of a balanced argument from 1–5 to show the order in which you should structure them.

☐ introduction ☐ title (question) ☐ points against ☐ points for ☐ conclusion

1 mark

3. Consider this question: *Should cars be banned from town and city centres?* Here are some arguments against this idea. Write four arguments for it.

for	against
	buses are expensive
	there aren't enough buses
	councils make money from car parks
	people feel safer in cars

4 marks

4. Turn the statement below into a question suitable as a title for a balanced argument.

Circuses should no longer use animal acts.

....

1 mark

5. Tick four of the conjunctions or phrases below that would help to link ideas within a single paragraph.

☐ firstly
☐ in addition
☐ on the other hand
☐ in conclusion
☐ for example
☐ consequently

2 marks

6. The conclusion sums up your argument. What else should it include?

....

1 mark

17 WRITING FICTION

1. Decide whether these sentence starters are in the first or third person. Then say whether they are in the past, present or future tense.

a) I was only nine when I saw an alien for the first time.

person:.. tense:..

b) The best thing about Uncle Angus is that he never gives up.

person:.. tense:..

c) "One day, I'll be the first person on Mars," Ellie declared.

person:.. tense:..

3 marks

2. Read the example and then make up your own 'story starter' sentence in the first person and the past tense.

Example: I should never have gone into the abandoned house.

....

1 mark

3. Number these plot elements from 1-5 in the order they should appear in a short story.

☐ solution ☐ opening ☐ build-up ☐ ending ☐ problem

1 mark

4. Tick <u>three</u> things you should decide before you start writing a fiction piece.

☐ the main characters
☐ the length
☐ the setting
☐ the conjunctions
☐ the mood

3 marks

5. Character descriptions should include details of what the person looks like and their personality (how they behave). Write two single-sentence character descriptions for the characters below. For example:

An adult: Mrs Treacle, a young teacher with brown curls, loved quizzes and building robots.

A child: ....

....

An old person: ....

....

2 marks

18 Nouns (Topic Test)

1. There are five common nouns and five proper nouns hidden in this word search, but the proper nouns are missing capital letters. Find all ten words and then sort them into the table below.

f	j	o	u	r	n	e	y	s	o
r	f	y	m	a	w	o	m	e	n
i	x	h	t	h	u	b	q	j	e
e	a	s	t	e	r	m	v	g	w
n	e	m	i	l	y	u	w	q	c
d	i	j	a	n	u	a	r	y	a
s	s	a	d	n	e	s	s	u	s
q	a	t	u	e	s	d	a	y	t
b	r	e	a	k	f	a	s	t	l
h	k	w	b	c	o	a	c	i	e

common nouns
proper nouns (add capital letters)

5 marks

2. Write out the noun phrases from the sentences below. One has been done for you.

a) It was a beautiful, sunny day.

beautiful, sunny day

b) When I saw him in the park earlier, he said he was on his way home.

c) The bottom of the hotel pool was covered in a thick layer of green slime.

d) Everybody in the family wanted to bake an enormous chocolate birthday cake.

3 marks

3. Rewrite the sentence below by expanding the noun phrases.

Every pet needs an owner.

2 marks

19 Pronouns and Determiners (Topic Test)

1. Rewrite the sentences below replacing the underlined words with suitable pronouns. One has been done for you.

a) Vikram bought a new smartphone. Vikram was pleased with the new smartphone.

Vikram bought a new smartphone. He was pleased with it.

b) Layla and I found some sweets. Layla and I ate all of the sweets.

....

c) Paloma was upset with me and Anabel. Actually, Paloma was really cross with me and Anabel.

....

2 marks

2. Circle all ten determiners in the cloud below.

yours it's them two hers
its an
some we your those
theirs the no
mine us him
another all I

5 marks

3. Circle all seven possessive pronouns in the passage below.

Your aunt Carolyn lives on her farm in Wales. My uncle George works on his farm next to hers. The farm next to that isn't theirs: it's ours!

1 mark

4. Which pair of possessive pronouns best completes the sentences below? Tick one.

a) We are leaving .... soon and we will arrive at .... this evening.

- ☐ mine, her
- ☐ his, my
- ☐ ours, theirs
- ☐ our, their

b) It's .... turn next and then it's ....

- ☐ their, our
- ☐ mine, yours
- ☐ my, their
- ☐ your, mine

2 marks

20 Adjectives and Adverbs

1. Complete the crossword below. All the answers are adjectives and antonyms of the clue words. One has been done for you.

Across
4. fortunate
5. strong
6. least
8. regular
9. lightest

Down
1. younger
2. boring
3. widest
7. best
10. quicker

4 marks

2. Underline the adjectives and circle the adverbs in the sentences below.

a) The fat cat stretched lazily on the carpet.

b) Lee, a thin builder, drove to work quickly and worked non-stop.

c) When I was younger, it was really exciting to go to the circus.

d) Mina got up very slowly and put on her crumpled red t-shirt.

4 marks

3. Rewrite the sentences below to move the adverbial to the start of the sentence.

a) There may be humans living on Mars fifty years from now. Who knows how far we will travel in the future?

....

....

b) Jodie was really thirsty after all the long speeches. She ordered a pint of water with ice and lemon at the bar.

....

....

2 marks

21 VERBS – PRESENT (TOPIC TEST)

1. Your friend tells you about a strange dream that they had. Underline all the present tense verbs and sort them into the three thought bubbles below.

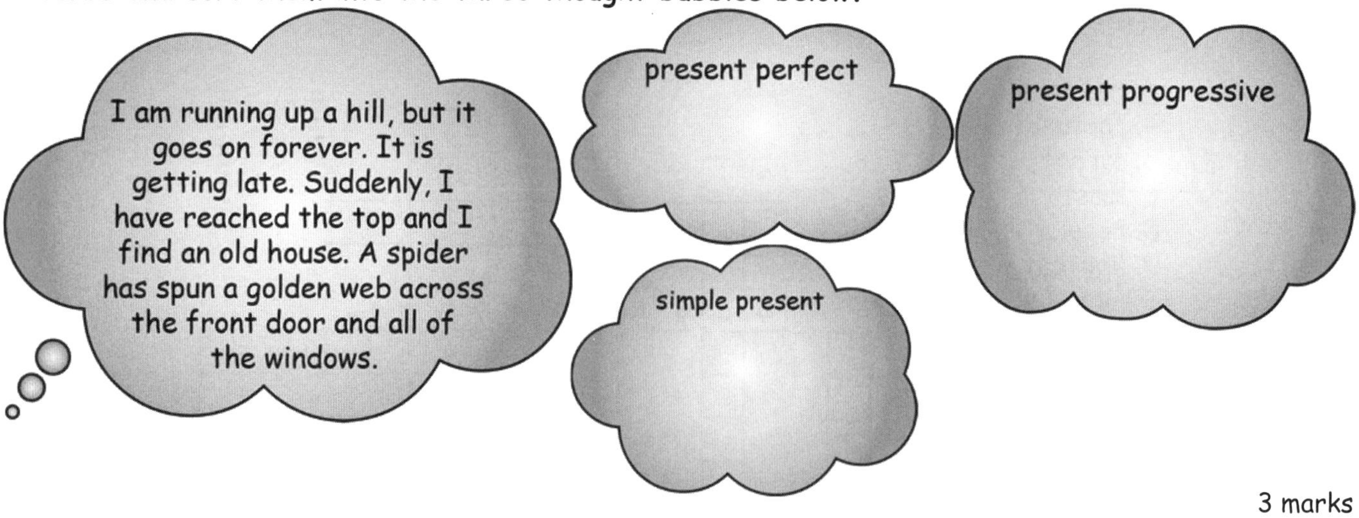

3 marks

2. Rewrite the sentences below changing the underlined verbs to the present perfect tense. One has been done for you.

a) The water is leaking and is freezing.

The water has leaked and has frozen.

b) A dog is chasing me and now it is licking me.

....

c) He drinks too many fizzy drinks and his teeth are falling out.

....

d) My family and I often visit France but we never fly.

....

3 marks

3. Complete the sentences below by using the form of the verb shown in brackets. One has been done for you.

a) We are swimming in a beautiful lake. (to swim – present progressive)

b) .... you .... that new sci-fi film? (to see – present perfect)

c) He .... even more powerful! (to become – present progressive)

d) I .... to your teacher. (to speak – present perfect)

e) They .... to understand. (to begin – present progressive)

4 marks

22 Verbs – past (topic test)

1. Circle all the past tense verbs in the passage below.

One day, dawn was breaking over the city. Suddenly, the earth shook violently and people were thrown off their feet. The main tremor lasted more than a minute. Nobody was killed during the earthquake, but many people were left homeless.

3 marks

2. Draw lines to match each sentence to the type of past tense verb used.

sentence
The tap was leaking.
I took the last bus home.
Connor had never seen a pantomime.

past tense verb
simple past
past perfect
past progressive

1 mark

3. Rewrite the sentences below, changing the verb from the past progressive to the simple past tense. One has been done for you.

a) We were going to the zoo.

We went to the zoo. ....

b) Dad was taking our dog to the vets.

....

c) My uncles were always forgetting my birthday.

....

d) The priest was lighting the candles.

....

3 marks

4. The tenses in the passage below are not used consistently. Rewrite the passage on a separate piece of paper, correcting the underlined verbs.

Last year, my family and I went to Egypt. We travel to Cairo and visited the famous museum. We saw Tutankhamun's golden death mask and some mummies. They have been incredible objects. We went to see the pyramids at Giza. The Sphinx was enormous. I will love it. We catch a train to Luxor. We will explore the Valley of the Kings. We don't find any new tombs though.

3 marks

23 VERBS – FUTURE AND MODAL (TOPIC TEST)

1. Write letters in each box to show whether the sentence is in the past tense, the present tense or the future tense.

Pa past	**Pr** present	**F** future

I am running quickly. ☐

Monty climbed a tall mountain. ☐

We will buy a boat at the beach. ☐

Evie's train leaves later on this evening ☐

My mum was laughing again. ☐

Laura is going to swim to France! ☐

My friend eats too much chocolate. ☐

3 marks

2. Underline the modal verb in the sentence below.

Would you like fish fingers for tea tonight?

1 mark

3. Here is a passage written by a historian. It is in the past tense. Read the passage and follow the instructions in the table below. Continue on another piece of paper if needed.

There was a great storm. The sea rose high up the beach. The water flooded the nearest houses. The village people had to run for their lives. The flood cut off the electricity. The streets were plunged into darkness. The situation was terrifying.

You are a fortune-teller! Rewrite the text putting the underlined verbs into the future tense.	**You are still a fortune-teller but this time you're not so confident about your predictions! Rewrite the text again, changing the underlined verbs to modal verbs.**
There will be a great storm.	There could be a great storm.
....	....
....	....
....	....
....	....
....	....
....	....

6 marks

24 Conjunctions and Prepositions (Topic Test)

1. The letters in the ten conjunctions below have been muddled up. Unscramble them and sort them into the table. One example of each has been done for you.

~~dan~~ ~~lihwe~~ ron casueeb iltnu tbu
huoghtla os lssenu tye ro evrewhne

co-ordinating conjunctions	subordinating conjunctions
and	while

2 marks

2. Circle the prepositions that are hidden on each line of this word search.

f	r	o	m	j	f	j	q	q	k
c	s	d	o	w	n	l	i	t	g
u	n	d	e	r	n	r	w	m	r
n	w	t	h	r	o	u	g	h	m
t	j	f	o	n	t	o	f	i	x
k	e	e	d	b	e	h	i	n	d
e	y	b	e	t	w	e	e	n	p
k	x	u	m	a	c	r	o	s	s
h	a	f	t	e	r	r	l	p	q
p	t	o	w	a	r	d	s	q	k

2 marks

3. Use appropriate conjunctions and prepositions from questions 1 and 2 to complete the sentences below. One has been done for you.

a) ......After...... tea, I went for a walk ......and...... bought some chips.

b) My little brother hides .... the table .... it's time for bed.

c) .... she's over 90, Lola's granny walked .... London to Paris.

d) The teacher is always firm .... fair .... everyone in the class.

6 marks

25 Sentence types (topic test)

1. Write a letter in each box to show the correct sentence type for each sentence below. One has been done for you.

S statement	**Q** question	**C** command	**E** exclamation

a) There are seven days in the week. [S]

b) Would you mind fetching the bucket for me? [ ]

c) Stop messing about and get on with your homework! [ ]

d) I don't know where I've put my car keys. [ ]

e) What a hot day it is today! [ ]

2 marks

2. Rewrite the questions below using a question tag. One has been done for you.

a) Are you making a cake?

You are making a cake, aren't you?

b) Is it time to water the garden?

....

c) Were we supposed meet up at the swimming pool?

....

1 mark

3. Underline the imperative verbs in the commands below.

a) Empty the bottle and fill it with fresh water.

b) When you hear the whistle, be quick and run towards the house.

1 mark

4. There are eight pieces of punctuation missing from the text below. Read the text and then add in the missing punctuation.

" Hurry up " shouted Dad . " You don't want to miss the start, do you "

I charged downstairs and sprinted to the car What was the time I glanced at my watch. We only had minutes to get there.

" Have you got everything " my mum asked I nodded.

Dad turned the key. Nothing happened Dad shook his head and said, " What a time for this to happen "

6 marks

26 Subject and Object

1. Underline the subject in each of the sentences below. One has been done for you.

a) The large dog barked aggressively at me.

b) Later that day, my grandmother and I went to buy some ice-cream.

c) Hidden behind a rock, it watched carefully as its prey approached.

1 mark

2. Underline the object in each of the sentences below. One has been done for you.

a) We are planning a special holiday this summer.

b) The old man donated all his money to charity.

c) I was chased home by a group of monkeys!

1 mark

3. Jonah has done the opposite of what he was asked to in his homework. Write the correct version of each of his sentences below.

a) Write an active sentence. Jonah's answer: *The moon was howled at by the wolf.*

Your correction:...

b) Write a passive sentence. Jonah's answer: *Mr Clark taught me to play rounders.*

Your correction:...

c) Write an active sentence. Jonah's answer: *We could have been washed away by the rising tide.*

Your correction:...

d) Write an active sentence. Jonah's answer: *The movie was completely ruined by a crying baby.*

Your correction:...

4 marks

4. Look at the sentences below and label the boxes with S (subject), V (verb) or O (object).

a) The stadium was destroyed by the storm.

☐ ☐ ☐

b) Our car was stolen during the night.

☐ ☐

2 marks

5. Write the passive forms of the active verbs below. One has been done for you.

a) blew → was blown

b) ate → ....

c) gave → ....

d) rode → ....

e) threw → ....

2 marks

27 Clauses (Topic Test)

1. Underline the main clause in each of the sentences below.
One has been done for you.

a) Stan wanted to learn to scuba-dive after he watched a nature documentary.

b) Four months earlier, just before summer, the Watsons had arrived in New York.

c) Vincent Starlight, who was an ageing rock star, couldn't find his electric guitar.

2 marks

2. Underline the subordinate clause in each of the sentences below.
One has been done for you.

a) My dad jogged every day until he was 80 years old.

b) Jerôme, who comes from Brittany in France, is staying with us for a few days.

c) While she was chasing a cat, my puppy fell into the pond.

2 marks

3. Rewrite the sentences below, swapping the positions of the main and subordinate clauses.
One has been done for you.

a) The shower was still not working even though the plumber had been.

Even though the plumber had been, the shower was still not working.

b) Unless we book early, we will never get tickets for the Olympics.

....

c) I always get woken up early whenever the birds start singing.

....

d) When she was on holiday in Spain, Meg twisted her ankle on a walk.

....

3 marks

4. a) Draw lines to match the main clause to the correct relative clause.

main clause
1. The old horse walked across the field.
2. The farmer was sad and confused.
3. My friend Patrick is going to America.
4. The parcel has gone missing.

relative clause
who once ate ten sausages
which was lame and almost blind
that was supposed to arrive today
whose sheep had disappeared

b) On a separate sheet of paper, rewrite 2-4 to include the relative clause in the right place.

3 marks

28 STANDARD ENGLISH (TOPIC TEST)

1. Circle the formal language in the cloud below.

In reference to your letter
Yo!
Yours sincerely
I would be grateful
LOL
Hey mate
Cheers
I'm well angry
In my opinion
See u later

2 marks

2. Circle the correct description for each sentence below. One has been done for you.

a) Me and my mate ain't done nothing.	Standard English	(non-Standard English)
b) Them burgers are legit sick.	Standard English	non-Standard English
c) My brother and I were late for school.	Standard English	non-Standard English
d) Isn't it strange that you like broccoli?	Standard English	non-Standard English
e) I could of helped earlier if you'd asked.	Standard English	non-Standard English

2 marks

3. Rewrite the passage below using Standard English.

Yesterday, me and Ben was soooo bored that we went to town. I seen some trainers what looked like a good deal but I didn't have no money cos I'd runned out. I phoned me mum. She says I should of saved up. I weren't happy.

....

....

....

....

....

6 marks

29 Basic Sentence Punctuation (Topic Test)

1. Circle the punctuation marks you can use to end a sentence.

? : . (! ;

1 mark

2. Add the correct verbs from the box below to turn the phrases into sentences. One has been done for you.

was blowing	disappeared	were melting	barked

a) a cold wind → A cold wind was blowing.

b) the pack of dogs → ....

c) eventually the sun → ....

d) all the delicious, creamy ice-creams → ....

3 marks

3. Rewrite the sentences below adding the correct punctuation. One has been done for you.

a) i've always wanted to go to Florida

I've always wanted to go to Florida.

b) why don't we go to the cinema this Friday

....

c) what an amazing experience that was

....

d) it's not fair why do I always get the blame

....

3 marks

4. Rewrite the passage below on a separate sheet of paper, inserting the missing punctuation.

"dad have you remembered that it's my birthday soon" I asked

dad sighed. "how could I forget you remind me every other day"

"well I was hoping you'd buy me some new boots," I said hopefully

"how much are they, darling" asked Mum

i hesitated and replied, "only two hundred pounds"

"what" roared Dad. "are you insane"

3 marks

30 Commas (Topic Test)

1. Rewrite the sentences below to place the subordinate clause first. Make sure you add a comma in the correct place. One has been done for you.

a) I go for a walk every day because it's good for my health.

Because it's good for my health, I go for a walk every day

b) We played in the mud for hours while it was pouring with rain.

....

c) I eat a whole bunch of bananas whenever I'm really hungry.

....

d) I'm going to do it unless you can persuade me otherwise.

....

3 marks

2. Rewrite these sentences with the commas in the correct places. One has been done for you.

a) Henry owned, a tablet a, laptop a PC, and a smartphone.

Henry owned a tablet, a, laptop, a PC and a smartphone.

b) Fred Tom, Joe Alistair, and Amir, are all coming to my party tomorrow.

....

c) Eliza who is, tall thin, and generous loves to, exercise read, and swim.

....

2 marks

3. Look at this sentence and add commas to the correct boxes.

Although Sara ☐ Maisie ☐ and Taya ☐ enjoyed netball ☐ they preferred ☐ playing basketball.

1 mark

4. Read the passage below, then add in the missing commas in the right places.

Just as Cameron was falling asleep there was a strange noise. He sat up sharply peered around the dark room listened carefully and then wondered if he had imagined it. He flopped back but then he heard it again. Although he didn't want to admit it it was clear someone else was in his room.

4 marks

31 PARENTHESIS (TOPIC TEST)

1. Look at this sentence and draw two brackets in the correct boxes to show where they should be placed.

A pair of brackets ☐ can be used ☐ for parenthesis ☐ just like in this sentence ☐.

1 mark

2. Add commas in the correct places in the sentences below to separate the relative clauses. One has been done for you.

a) The woman, who was holding a handbag, quickly rushed out of the shop.

b) Many people especially people who are old struggle to use computers.

c) My cousin whose friend is a movie star is taking me to a film premiere.

d) Gordon who is an experienced mountaineer climbed to the summit in record time.

e) An old sports car which made an incredible noise was on show at the fair.

4 marks

3. Draw lines to match each sentence to the extra information you could add to it.

sentence
Sir Francis Drake was a famous Tudor sea captain.
The opera was long and boring.
The Nile Crocodile can grow up to 6 metres long.
The stranger was listening to our conversation.
My uncle can't wear ordinary shoes.

extra information
a short man with dark hair
1540-1596
the one with the extra toe
which I was forced to watch
Crocodylus niloticus

4. On a separate piece of paper, write each sentence out. Add the extra information in a suitable place and separate it with a pair of commas, brackets or dashes.

5 marks

32 COLONS AND SEMI-COLONS (TOPIC TEST)

1. For each sentence below, write a colon (:) in the correct box.

a) I am ☐ really hungry ☐ I haven't eaten anything ☐ since breakfast.

b) Lula got ☐ what she wanted ☐ her mum ☐ gave her a fluffy scarf for winter.

2 marks

2. For each sentence below, write a semi-colon (;) in the correct box.

a) Send me a text tomorrow ☐ I'll let you know ☐ where we are ☐ meeting up.

b) When we play rugby, I love chasing ☐ and tackling ☐ you prefer ☐ dodging and kicking.

2 marks

3. Rewrite the sentences below, adding colons and commas in the correct places.
One has been done for you.

a) Yesterday I saw an eagle a hawk a vulture and a buzzard.

Yesterday I saw: an eagle, a hawk, a vulture and a buzzard.

b) Marco loved cooked breakfasts sausages beans a fried egg and bacon.

....

....

c) The following items are for sale a cot some blankets cuddly toys and a pram.

....

....

d) On holiday in Greece we visited a canyon in Crete called the Samaria Gorge the ancient theatre of Delphi and the Parthenon on top of the Acropolis in Athens.

....

....

e) At the Chinese restaurant, I ordered a bowl of delicious sweet and sour pork a plate of vegetable dumplings stir-fried chicken noodles and Peking duck in pancakes.

....

....

6 marks

33 Apostrophes

1. Rewrite the phrases below using an apostrophe to show possession. One has been done for you.

the ladder belonging to my dad .... my dad's ladder

the birthday belonging to Boris ....

the shoes belonging to the women ....

the headphones belonging to the boys ....

the quacking belonging to the ducks ....

the toys belonging to the children ....

3 marks

2. Rewrite each of the contractions below in their uncontracted form to reveal the hidden word in the puzzle.

1. I'm
2. who's
3. wasn't
4. it's
5. we're
6. doesn't
7. she'd
8. we've

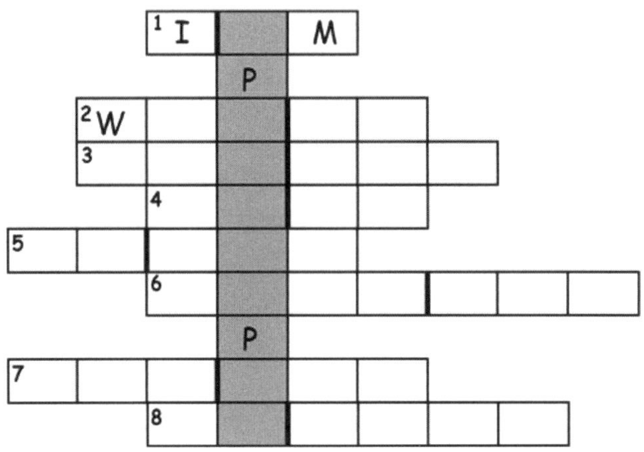

4 marks

3. Rewrite the sentences below, moving the apostrophes to the correct places and removing any that are incorrect. One has been done for you.

a) Whats' the weather going to be like on Tues'day at four oc'lock?

What's the weather going to be like on Tuesday at four o'clock?

b) I shouldv'e taken Yasmins' thing's to her earlier.

....

c) Whys' it alway's your brothe'rs turn on the console?

....

d) I'tll be soon be too late to save Mikes' lost animals'.

....

3 marks

34 PUNCTUATING SPEECH (TOPIC TEST)

1. Rewrite the sentences below, moving the punctuation to the correct places. One has been done for you.

a) It is "time for tea", said. Mum

"It is time for tea," said Mum.

b) Brendan whispered ",You will never get away with this"!

....

c) Why don't "you" buy a new one. asked my friend?

....

d) "We are not too late" There. is still time. urged Katie!

....

3 marks

2. Rewrite the sentences below, adding all the punctuation needed for direct speech.

a) You could start a new hobby suggested my mum.

....

b) Talvinder said Isn't it great The holidays start tomorrow

....

2 marks

3. Rewrite the passage below, changing the direct speech to reported speech and the reported speech to direct speech.

Thomas asked, "How long will it take to get there?" I told him that it would take at least three hours. "But I'm bored already," he moaned. I suggested that he should read his book or play on his phone. "But I get carsick if I do that," he reminded me.

....

....

....

....

....

5 marks

35 Hyphens and Single Dashes (Topic Test)

1. a) Tick one box in each row to show whether the sentences need hyphens, a single dash or both at the places indicated. One has been done for you.

Sentence	hyphen	single dash	both
The middle ....aged woman feels re ....energised.	✓		
The film was fantastic .... but then I like anything!			
Do you want a full ....time or a part .... time job?			
My father .... in ....law seems nice ....or is he?			

1 mark

b) On a separate sheet of paper, write out each sentence correctly. One has been done for you.

The middle-aged woman feels re-energised.

2 marks

2. Match the words to make compound adjectives and then write them in the correct row to describe the nouns. One has been done for you.

~~strange~~	watering	a ....strange-looking......... person
little	~~looking~~	a ....fact
man	provoking	a .... tiger
twenty	known	a ....building
English	minute	an ....country
last	lasting	a ....warning
long	speaking	a .... friendship
mouth	eating	a ....choice of puddings
thought	storey	a ....documentary

4 marks

3. Read the sentences below and then add in hyphens and single dashes where they are needed.

a) My twelve year old son is really funny at least, I think so.

b) My instructor said I'll need self discipline to re educate my body and mind.

c) Dad is going to be forty two next week sorry, I mean forty three.

3 marks

36 WORD FAMILIES (TOPIC TEST)

1. Underline the root word in each of the words below.

information formative transformers conformation formality

1 mark

2. Write antonyms for the words below by adding the correct prefixes. One has been done for you.

a) obey → disobey ....

b) logical → ....

c) patient → ....

d) spell → ....

e) known → ....

2 marks

3. Write adjectives for the words below by adding the appropriate suffixes. One has been done for you.

a) help → helpful ....

b) education → ....

c) fantasy → ....

d) sense → ....

e) ambition → ....

2 marks

4. Rewrite the passage below, putting all of the underlined nouns into the plural form.

It was a very strange place: someone had abandoned the piano in the alley; the woman had left the child and baby; the chef used the knife to prepare the strawberry; and the kangaroo bounded over the roof.

....

....

....

....

....

....

5 marks

37 SYNONYMS, ANTONYMS AND HOMOPHONES (TOPIC TEST)

1. **Sort the words in the bubble into the correct columns in the table below.**

synonyms	antonyms	homophones
bright/clever		

3 marks

2. **Write homophones for each of the words below. One has been done for you.**

a) piece → peace ....

b) here → ....

c) weather → ....

d) to → ....

e) there → ....

3 marks

3. **Complete the crossword below using synonyms, antonyms or homophones of the clues.**

<u>Across</u>
3. war (antonym)
5. aloud (homophone)
7. similar (antonym)
9. children (antonym)
10. witch (homophone)

<u>Down</u>
1. generous (antonym)
2. warrior (synonym)
4. led (homophone)
6. rich (synonym)
8. wound (synonym)

4 marks

38 Tricky spellings (topic test)

1. a) Circle the words below that are spelled correctly.

gohst psychic weird diffrent
thorough believe avridge Wednsday

b) Write the correct spelling of the words that you haven't circled.

....

....

2 marks

2. Write the correct spellings for each of these words. One has been done for you.

a) ruff ....rough..........   b) nives ....

c) acheivement ....   d) intrested ....

e) enviroment ....

2 marks

3. Underline the only incorrect spelling in this word snake.

1 mark

4. Complete the crossword below. Remember these are tricky spellings and the puzzle will only work if you spell the words correctly.

Across
4. a soldier from fairy tales
5. a building with a collection of books
7. a body tissue that produces movement
9. a plant grown to be eaten
10. a farming tool with blades to dig soil

Down
1. a mix of flour and water for making bread
2. a piece of land used by farmers
3. a type of fuel
6. to think something is true
8. the surface of a room above your head

5 marks

PRACTICE PAPERS

On the following pages, you will find a set of practice papers modelled on the sample assessment material and past papers provided by the government. It comprises a reading booklet, a reading answer booklet, a grammar and punctuation test and a spelling test. The booklet includes space for your student's answers.

If you want to see how your student performs in test conditions, provide a quiet working environment, adhere to the timings given on each paper and answer questions relating to the practicalities of the test only.

ENGLISH READING TEST

Reading booklet

The reading booklet contains three texts: one fiction, one non-fiction and one poem. These texts provide the target information for the questions in the reading answer booklet, and should be read carefully by the student. Note that the test students sit at the end of Year 6 may not have exactly three texts, but will have approximately the same amount of reading material.

Reading answer booklet

The reading answer booklet comprises 36 questions, worth a total of 50 marks. The test should take one hour to complete, including reading time. The student can approach the test as they choose. They may wish to read one text and answer all of its the questions before moving on to the next text. The student will encounter a variety of question types, requiring selected answers, short answers and long answers. More information about question types and their associated demands can be found on pages 7–8. The mark scheme for the reading paper can be found on page 162.

ENGLISH GRAMMAR, PUNCTUATION AND SPELLING TEST

Paper 1: questions

The student will have 45 minutes to complete the grammar, punctuation and spelling question paper, which will include 49 questions worth a total of 50 marks. Some questions require multiple-choice answers and some require short written answers, covering a range of grammar, punctuation and spelling skills. More information about question types and their associated demands can be found on pages 7–8. The answers and mark allocation can be found on page 167.

Paper 2: spelling

This component of the test consists of an answer booklet for the student to complete and a test transcript for you to read to the student. The spelling paper comprises 20 sentences with 20 missing words worth one mark each. The test will take approximately 15 minutes, during which you will read the sentences out loud and the student will attempt to spell the missing words correctly. You do not need to time this test strictly. The script for the spelling test is available on page 173 and the mark scheme and content domain information can be found on page 174. The student should not make use of a dictionary or any other spell checker in the test.

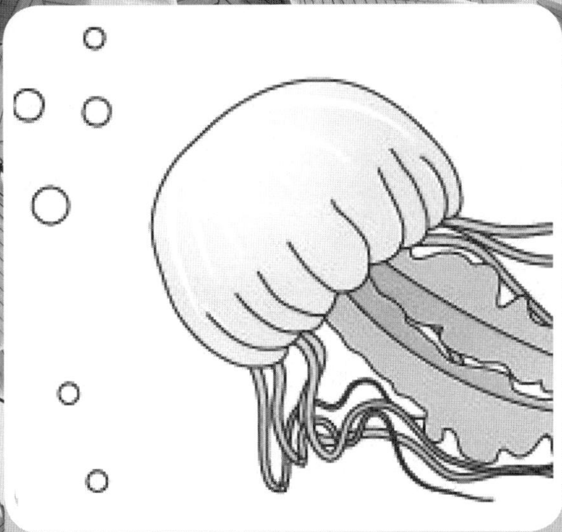

Jellyfish

The Heron's Feather

The Fieldmouse

Reading Booklet

Contents

JELLYFISH

Why do we call these beautiful creatures jellyfish?

They're not made of jelly, and they're not even fish! They're actually classified as a sort of plankton, but although most plankton are tiny water-dwelling creatures less than two centimetres across, some jellyfish can grow to more than one metre in diameter. The main reason we call them jellyfish is that their blobby bodies look and move a bit like jelly.

Inside a jellyfish

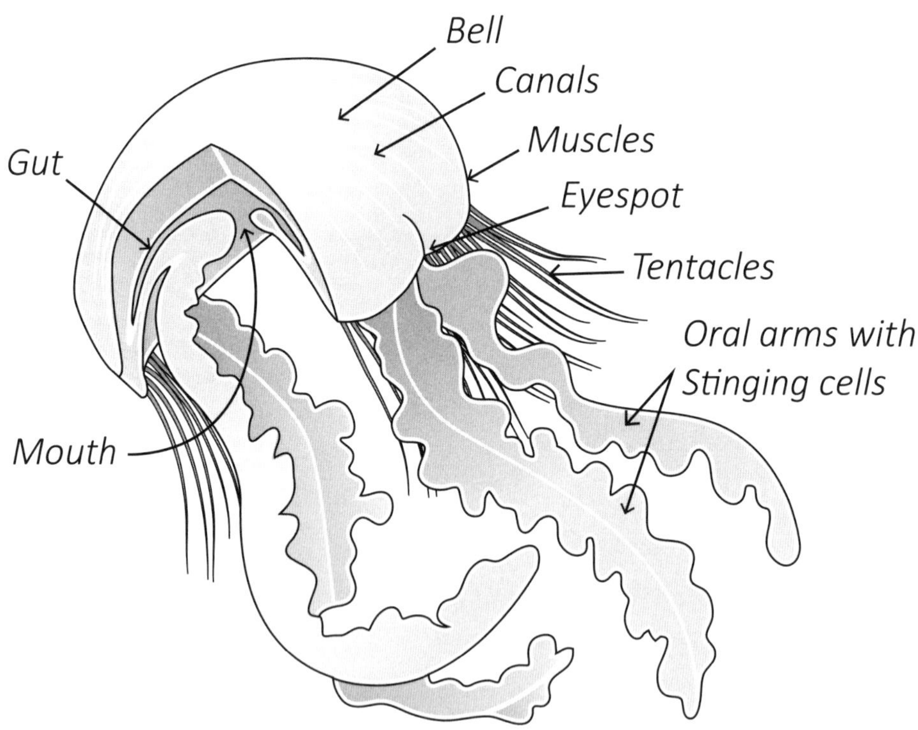

Unlike many animals, jellyfish are often transparent, so you can actually see inside them without an X-ray. However, if you spot one in the sea, it's not always easy to identify the different parts of a jellyfish. This diagram shows the parts of a 'true' jellyfish of the type called *Scyphozoa*.

You can see from the diagram that jellyfish are a lot more complicated than jelly! However, they are still quite simple animals. Jellyfish don't have bones or any big internal structures to make them stiff.

They don't have brains, a heart or any blood, either. Jellyfish are made of about 95 per cent water, and they also contain a lot of protein which makes the watery bits wobble. Actually, this is another way in which jellyfish are a bit like edible jelly. The jelly we eat is also mostly made up of water plus protein in the form of something like gelatine, which makes the jelly wobbly.

How jellyfish move

If you have ever seen jellyfish in the sea, or in an aquarium, you will know that they can move in a very graceful, almost magical way. They move by pulsing their bodies in the water. The movement sends out a spurt of water from their body cavity, which propels the jellyfish through the water.

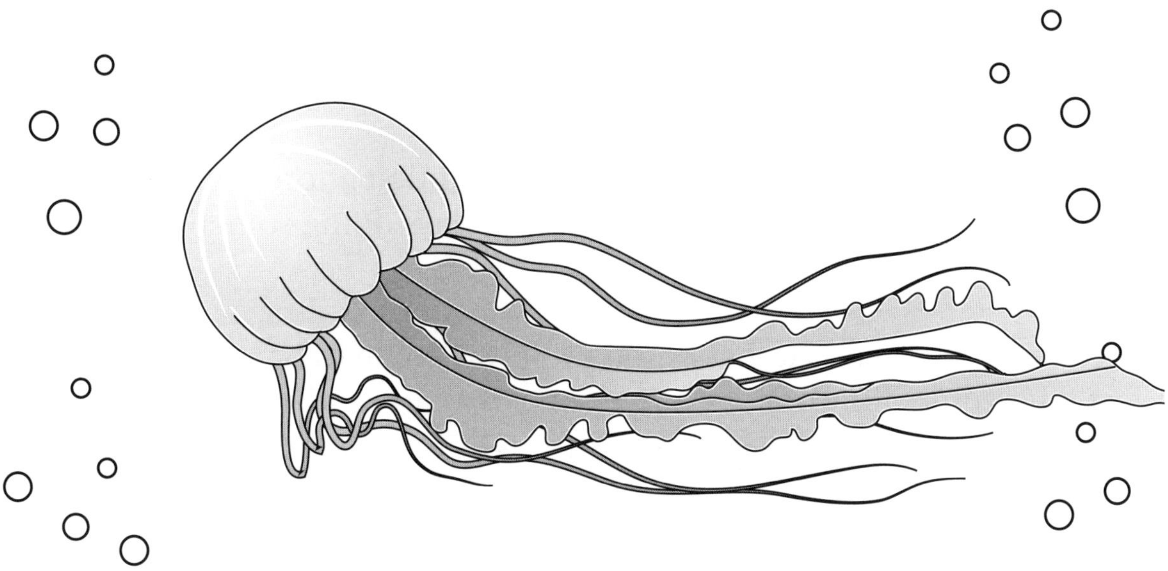

Some types of jellyfish are edible, and in some places around the world, people do enjoy eating them! For example, when the fishing town of Obama in Japan was suffering from a plague of slimy Nomura jellyfish nearly two metres wide, local people decided to fight back. They began turning the jellyfish into stews, sushi and other tasty meals. Jellyfish is also popular in some parts of China, where it is often regarded as a delicacy.

You may not be keen on the idea of tucking into a plateful of jellyfish and chips, but who knows? As the world's population increases in the future and we have to look for new sources of food, more and more of us might find jellyfish on the menu!

The Heron's Feather

In this extract, Casey is on holiday with her mum and sister.

I've just seen something really strange.

We're camping at a place called Brazeberrow Farm. It's only about ten miles from home, but it feels like the other side of the world – just an empty field, no Wi-Fi, no other kids to play with. There isn't even a shower or a proper loo. There's nothing around us but woods and fields. Apparently there's a Bronze Age burial site around here somewhere, but it's got to be the most boring ancient monument ever, because there's nothing left of it that you can actually see.

It was Mum's idea to come here; she told us she couldn't afford a proper holiday this year, but at least we could have a few days doing something different.

Well, it's certainly different! At first I thought it was going to be really boring, but in fact it was quite fun cooking supper on a real fire, and snuggling down to sleep in the tent with all the sounds of the night-time world still going on around us.

It's actually not that easy to sleep in a tent. The noises are a bit weird at first – owls hooting, trees rustling, and who knows what kinds of animals snuffling round the edges of the tent in the darkness. Then, early in the morning, the sun shines yellow through the tent's canvas and you find you're awake whether you want to be or not.

So this morning, while Mum and Martha were still snoring, I wriggled quietly out of the tent and stood in the field all by myself. Everything was still and calm, with the faintest mist rising up from the stream at the bottom of the field.

Suddenly a huge bird took off, flapping clumsily over my head like a broken umbrella. Once it had gained a bit of height, though, it soared away like the most graceful creature in the world. I watched it till it was out of sight – and then I saw someone watching me, from the field on the other side of the stream.

It was a boy about my age. At first I thought he was a girl, because he seemed to be wearing a sort of rough woollen dress over trousers. He had a long spear in one hand, and for a moment I thought he was going to throw it at me, but he lowered his hand and just looked at me. I looked back at him, and I couldn't think what to say. Still staring at me, he pulled a long grey feather out of his hair and laid it down carefully on the ground near his feet. Then he vanished. I don't think he ran away – I didn't see him move at all – it's just that suddenly he wasn't there.

I thought I must have dreamed the whole thing, but when I splashed across the stream to check, I found the long grey feather lying just where the boy had placed it. I picked it up and, without even thinking, stuck it in my own hair.

I don't know what I just saw, but I can tell you one thing – I'm going back there tomorrow morning. Perhaps I'll see the strange boy again; who knows?

* * *

There's a sprite living in the field on the other side of the stream! Mother says I'm maze-headed, but I know it's true – I've seen it. I was off hunting at first light this morning when I saw it standing there, looking at me as if I were the sprite, not it. I was frightened at first, but I don't think it wanted to hurt me. Just to be safe, though, I took my special heron feather out of my hair and left it as a peace offering. I think it's a friendly sprite. I wish it could speak to me, and then we might be friends together. Maybe, if I go back tomorrow morning, it will still be there.

The Fieldmouse

by Cecil Frances Alexander

Where the acorn tumbles down,
Where the ash tree sheds its berry,
With your fur so soft and brown,
With your eye so round and merry,
Scarcely moving the long grass,
Fieldmouse, I can see you pass.
Little thing, in what dark den,
Lie you all the winter sleeping?
Till warm weather comes again,
Then once more I see you peeping
Round about the tall tree roots,
Nibbling at their fallen fruits.

Fieldmouse, fieldmouse, do not go,
Where the farmer stacks his treasure,
Find the nut that falls below,
Eat the acorn at your pleasure,
But you must not steal the grain
He has stacked with so much pain.
Make your hole where mosses spring,
Underneath the tall oak's shadow,
Pretty, quiet, harmless thing,
Play about the sunny meadow.
Keep away from corn and house,
None will harm you, little mouse.

[Blank page]
Please do not write on this page.

Reading answer booklet

Instructions

Questions and answers

This paper contains questions about the texts in the Reading booklet.

You have **one hour** to read the texts and answer the questions.

There are three texts. Read one text and answer the questions about it before moving on to the next one.

There are three types of question. Each type of question needs a different type of answer:

Selected answer

For these questions, you do not need to write anything. Instead, you might need to tick a box, draw lines or circle an answer. Read the instructions carefully so you know what to do.

Short answer

These questions have one or two answer lines. You need to write a word, a few words or a short sentence in your answer.

Long answer

These questions have several answer lines. You need to write a longer, more detailed answer to explain your opinion.

Marks

The number at the side of the page tells you the maximum number of marks for each question.

Work through this answer booklet until you are told to stop. Go back to the Reading booklet whenever you need to. If a question includes a page number, go back to that page to help you with your answer.

Questions 1–12 are about *Jellyfish* (pages 91–92).

1 How are jellyfish different from most plankton?

Tick **one**.

Unlike plankton, jellyfish live in the sea. ☐

Jellyfish are a different colour from plankton. ☐

Unlike jellyfish, plankton are made of jelly. ☐

Jellyfish can grow much bigger than most plankton. ☐

1 mark

2 Find and copy **two** things that jellyfish have in common with edible jelly.

1.____

2. ____

2 marks

3 Which part of its body does a jellyfish use to sting things? Circle **one**.

its mouth | its tentacles | its oral arms | its canals

1 mark

4 Do you think the author of this article likes the idea of eating jellyfish? Use evidence from the text to support your answer.

____

____

____

____

2 marks

5 Where is a jellyfish's brain?

	Tick **one**.
in its gut	☐
behind its eyespot	☐
it doesn't have one	☐
inside its bell	☐

1 mark

6

They move by pulsing their bodies in the water, and the movement sends out a spurt of water from their body cavity which propels the jellyfish through the water.

Which word or phrase could replace *propels the jellyfish* in this sentence?

Circle **one**.

scatters the jellyfish | sends the jellyfish forward

stops the jellyfish moving | makes the jellyfish disappear

1 mark

7

Why do you think the author included a diagram in this text?
Give **two** reasons.

____

____

____

____

2 marks

8

Find and copy **one** word on page 92 that means the same as *slippery*.

____

1 mark

9 Write a subheading for the last two paragraphs of the text.

Your subheading should sum up the main idea in these paragraphs.

____

1 mark

10 *Jellyfish is also popular in some parts of China, where it is often regarded as a delicacy.*

Which word most closely matches the meaning of the word *delicacy*?

Tick **one**.

medicine ☐

treat ☐

side-dish ☐

everyday meal ☐

1 mark

11 Explain in your own words how the shape of a jellyfish's body helps it to move.

____

____

1 mark

12 Find and copy **one** phrase from the text that is intended to make the reader think of jellyfish as unpleasant or threatening.

____

1 mark

Questions 13–25 are about *The Heron's Feather* (pages 93–94).

13 What did the narrator, Casey, think camping would be like at first?

Tick **one**.

exciting ☐

boring ☐

frightening ☐

dangerous ☐

1 mark

14 *I've just seen something really strange.*

(a) Why do you think the author chose to start the story with this sentence? Explain your reasons.

____

____

1 mark

(b) Do you think this makes an effective opening for the story? Explain your reasons.

____

____

1 mark

15 Why had Casey's family gone on a camping holiday? Circle **one**.

because it was quite cheap	because Casey's sister loved camping
because it was near where Mum worked	because the weather was so nice

1 mark

16 What did Casey enjoy about camping?

Tick **two**.

- having no access to the Internet ☐
- not needing to have a shower ☐
- cooking on a campfire ☐
- swimming in the river ☐
- settling down for the night in the tent ☐

1 mark

17 *Apparently there's a Bronze Age burial site around here somewhere …*

Why does the author tell the reader this piece of information?

Explain in your own words how this fact becomes relevant later in the story.

____

____

____

2 marks

18 Find and copy the word that tells you whether Casey's mum was asleep when Casey left the tent.

____

1 mark

19 Complete the table to show how you think Casey felt at different points in the story. Use evidence from the text to support your answer.

	How did Casey feel?	Evidence
When she first saw the campsite ...		
When she was watching the huge bird in flight ...		
When she first saw the strange boy ...		

3 marks

20 What can you infer about the boy that Casey sees? Explain who you think he is. Use evidence from the text to support your answer.

____

____

____

____

2 marks

21 Below is a map of the area where Casey and her family are camping.
Write *Casey* on the map to show where Casey is standing when she sees the boy, and write *boy* to show where the boy is standing.

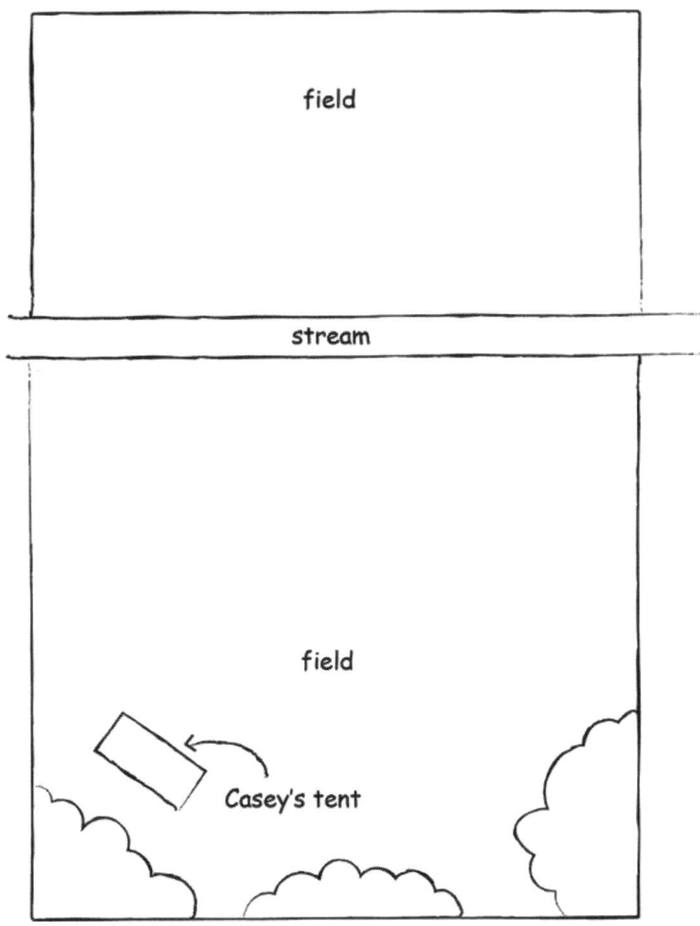

1 mark

22 *...it's got to be the most boring ancient monument ever*

Which phrase most closely matches the meaning of the word *monument*?

Tick **one**.

a building of historical importance ☐

an old-fashioned thing ☐

a field ☐

a tourist attraction ☐

1 mark

23 Write an alternative title for this story that summarises its theme.

____

1 mark

24 Read the last paragraph.

(a) Why has the author used *italic* text for this paragraph?

____

____

1 mark

(b) Who is the narrator of this paragraph?

____

1 mark

(c) Find and copy **two** unusual words that the narrator of this paragraph uses. Write a definition for each of these words below. You can use the meaning of the sentences around them to help you work out what the words mean.

____

____

____

1 mark

25 What do you think will happen the next morning? Remember to make your prediction fit with the rest of the story.

____

____

1 mark

Questions 26–36 are about *The Fieldmouse* (pages 95–96).

26 Who is this poem addressed to?

Tick **one**.

the fieldmouse ☐

the poet ☐

the farmer ☐

the reader ☐

1 mark

27 Read lines 1–6. What time of year is it? Use evidence from the text to support your answer.

____

____

____

2 marks

28 How does the poet describe the fieldmouse's appearance?

____

____

____

1 mark

29

Scarcely moving the long grass,

Fieldmouse, I can see you pass.

(a) Give the meaning of the word *scarcely* in this sentence.

____

1 mark

(b) What do these lines suggest about how the fieldmouse moves?

____

1 mark

30

Fieldmouse, fieldmouse, do not go

Where the farmer stacks his treasure

In this line, explain what the poet means by the farmer's *treasure*.

____

____

1 mark

31 (a) What does the poet tell the fieldmouse *not* to take?

Tick **one**.

valuables ☐

crops ☐

buildings ☐

acorns ☐

1 mark

(b) Why does the poet feel it would be wrong of the fieldmouse to eat this?

Use evidence from the poem to support your answer.

____

____

____

1 mark

32 Find and copy **one** word that has a similar meaning to *corn*.

____

1 mark

33 Draw lines to match the questions with the correct answers from the poem.

Where does the fieldmouse sleep?	*Nibbling at their fallen fruits*
What does the fieldmouse eat?	*In what dark den*
Where shouldn't the fieldmouse go?	*Underneath the tall oak's shadow*
Where should the fieldmouse live?	*Where the farmer stacks his treasure*

1 mark

34 In your own words, explain what might happen if the fieldmouse ignored the poet's advice. Use evidence from the poem to support your answer.

____

____

____

1 mark

35 Complete the table with evidence to show how the poet changes the reader's opinion of the fieldmouse at different points in the poem.

Reader's opinion	Quote from the text
The mouse is naughty.	
The mouse is good.	

2 marks

36 Read the last two lines of the poem. Do you think they are a satisfying ending to the poem? Explain your reasons.

___

___

___

1 mark

Grammar, punctuation and spelling: questions

Instructions

Questions and answers

This paper contains questions about grammar, punctuation and spelling.

You have **45 minutes** to answer the questions.

There are two types of question. Each type of question needs a different types of answer:

Multiple-choice answers

For some questions, you do not need to do any writing. Read the instructions carefully so that you know how to answer each question.

Short answers

Some questions are followed by a line or a box. This shows that you need to write a word, a few words or a sentence.

Marks

The number at the side of the page tells you the maximum number of marks for each question.

Work through this answer booklet until you are told to stop. Work as quickly and as carefully as you can. If you finish before the end, go back and check your work.

1 Circle the **conjunction** in the sentence below.

Tom kicked a stone along the pavement while he waited for his mum to finish shopping.

1 mark

2 Replace the underlined word or words in each sentence below with the correct **pronoun**.

When Lina's brothers saw <u>Lina</u> coming, <u>Lina's brothers</u> ran away.

[ ] [ ]

1 mark

Asif sat down on <u>Asif's</u> chair so fast that <u>Asif's chair</u> fell over.

[ ] [ ]

1 mark

3 Which sentence below uses the **semi-colon** correctly?

Tick **one**.

My dad loves fishing he once caught a massive pike; with razor-sharp teeth. ☐

My dad loves fishing; he once caught a massive pike with razor-sharp teeth. ☐

My dad loves fishing he once caught; a massive pike with razor-sharp teeth. ☐

My dad loves fishing he once caught a massive; pike with razor-sharp teeth. ☐

1 mark

4 Tick one box in each row to show whether the **inverted commas** are used correctly in the sentences below.

Sentence	Inverted commas used correctly	Inverted commas used incorrectly
"Listen, said Ola," "I've got something important to tell you."		
"Chocolate cake is my favourite, said Marco dreamily."		
"How many times do I have to tell you? said Mrs Fisher." Just sit down and wait quietly!		
"Deep in the heart of the jungle," said the guide, "there's a very rare white lion."		

1 mark

5 Circle the **modal verb** in each sentence below.

I might come round after tea today.

Do you think I should paint my bedroom black?

We will go and have lunch with Gran next Sunday.

Whatever you do, you must see the new spy film – it's amazing!

1 mark

6 Add the correct **prefix** to each verb below, so that it means the opposite.

__________ understand

__________ appear

__________ tie

__________ behave

1 mark

7 Which of the sentences below is a **statement**?

Tick **one**.

You have always loved the colour red, haven't you ☐

What an enormous birthday cake ☐

Far, far below the surface of the lake, something gigantic started to move ☐

Don't be silly ☐

1 mark

8 Which **punctuation mark** should be used in the place indicated by the arrow in the sentence below?

Mr Webster's favourite colour is grey
↑

Tick **one**.

colon ☐

exclamation mark ☐

full stop ☐

question mark ☐

1 mark

9

Tick one box in each row to show whether each sentence below is written in **Standard English** or **non-Standard English.**

Sentence	Standard English	Non-Standard English
The sunflowers that we planted in the spring are taller than me now.		
The dog what stole our ball ran out of the park.		
Gran told me what she wanted from the shops.		
The bus what goes into town takes a really long time.		

1 mark

10

Rewrite the sentence below so that it is in **Standard English**.

Mum were tired, so I done all the washing up.

____

1 mark

11 Rearrange the words in the question below to make it a **statement**. Use only the given words. Remember to punctuate your sentence.

Question: Have you finished eating your sandwich?

Statement:

____

1 mark

12 Draw a line to match each **sentence** to its correct **function**.

Sentence
Have you ever tasted anything as delicious as this soup
My soup is a bit cold
What a strange colour the soup is
Sit down and eat your soup

Function
exclamation
command
question
statement

1 mark

13 Complete the sentence below with an appropriate **adverb**.

At home time, we all left the classroom ________________.

1 mark

14 Underline the **adjectives** and draw circles around the **adverbs** in the sentence below.

The slimy monster opened its enormous mouth hungrily, and its long green tentacles swung around wildly.

1 mark

15

Complete the sentence below by writing the **conjunctions** from the box in the correct places. Use each conjunction only **once**.

so	because	while

I got bored ________________ I was waiting for Ali, ________________

it took him ages to get changed, ________________ I went home

with Tom.

1 mark

16

Write an appropriate **determiner** in each gap to complete the sentences in this story.

On my way home after school, I saw ________________ massive

dinosaur crossing the road. Mrs Fisher was riding on ________________

dinosaur's back. She gave me ________________ friendly wave. It was

________________ amazing sight.

1 mark

17 Circle all the **possessive pronouns** in the sentence below.

Michael knew that he shouldn't have taken his sister's bike without asking her, but his bike had a puncture, and hers was just the right size for him to ride.

1 mark

18 Underline the **subordinate clause** in each sentence below.

We went to the park after we had finished all the shopping.

Alex and I went swimming, while Mum and Nan sunbathed.

After his exhausting day, Jamie went straight to bed.

Because you kindly shared your crisps with me, I will give you a lick of my ice-cream.

1 mark

19

Tick one box in each row to show which sentences have a **co-ordinating conjunction**, and which of the sentences below have a **subordinating conjunction**.

Sentence	Co-ordinating conjunction	Subordinating conjunction
We sat on the harbour wall and ate our fish and chips.		
The seagulls tried to steal our chips, but we scared them off.		
When we had finished our meal, we decided to go to the fairground.		
Jess regretted going on the big dipper, because she felt a bit sick.		

1 mark

20

Underline the **noun phrase** in each of the sentences below. In the box next to each sentence, write **two** appropriate **adjectives** to expand the noun phrase.

The dog was growling.

I've never seen such a mess!

Fortunately, I had a plan.

1 mark

21 What does the **root word** 'photo' mean in the word family below?

photograph   photocopier   microphotography   photosynthesis

Tick **one**.

sound ☐

writing ☐

light ☐

science ☐

1 mark

22 Which two sentences below use the **present perfect** form?

Tick **two**.

Bella has lost her PE kit. ☐

We were all exhausted because it was such a hot day. ☐

Ted and Sanjit have spotted some baby birds in the nest in the big tree. ☐

It is too cold to go swimming. ☐

1 mark

23 Underline all the **modal verbs** in the sentences below.

I could never dive from the top board – I would be too scared!

You may go swimming with Tom, but you must remember your goggles.

Rani might come to the cinema with us if she gets home in time.

You should let your little sister play, as otherwise she might start crying, and then your mum would get cross.

1 mark

24 Which verb completes the sentence below so that it uses the **subjunctive** form?

If I ________________ the ruler of the world, everyone would have chips for breakfast.

Tick **one**.

am ☐

was ☐

were ☐

be ☐

1 mark

25 The words below are either **synonyms** or **antonyms** of the word 'small'. Draw lines to show which words are synonyms and which words are antonyms.

tiny		
enormous		
minute		synonym
gigantic		
towering		
huge		antonym
little		
microscopic		

1 mark

26 Explain how the different **prefixes** change the meanings of the two sentences below.

Zac disarranged the cushions on the sofa.

This means that Zac ...

____

Zac rearranged the cushions on the sofa.

This means that Zac ...

____

1 mark

27

Rewrite the **informal** sentence below so that it contains the same information but sounds more **formal**.

I reckon there are loads of kids who'd be well chuffed to get an invite to a swimming party.

____

____

1 mark

28

Tick one box in each row to show whether each of the sentences below uses **capital letters** correctly.

Sentence	Capitals used correctly	Capitals used incorrectly
After School on Wednesday we went to broadcliffe downs park.		
Martha and jamie have been friends since they were Five years old.		
Although I've never been to Paris, I've heard that the view from the top of the Eiffel Tower is amazing.		
We go to visit gran on Wednesdays and Fridays, but not usually at the Weekend.		

1 mark

29 Rewrite the sentence below, adding the correct **punctuation.**

At my party we ate pizza garlic bread carrot sticks grapes and cake and we drank lemonade water and cola

____

____

1 mark

30 Insert **one comma** in the correct place in the sentence below.

Blotting out the sun with its magnificent wings the dragon rose into the sky.

1 mark

31 Tick two of the boxes to show where the missing **inverted commas** should go in the sentence below.

☐ I'm amazed you can manage a piece of cake after all that pizza, ☐ said

☐ Grandad ☐ admiringly.

1 mark

32 Which of these sentences uses **commas to indicate parenthesis** correctly?

Tick **one**.

My dog Harry who is, the bravest animal I know, took one look at the goose and ran away. ☐

In the cupboard under the stairs, just behind the vacuum cleaner, lived a tiny goblin. ☐

I saw the bus coming and I'm sure the driver saw me, but it didn't stop to let me, and my sister on. ☐

After lunch just as I was settling down to read my book, my big brother, Toby came in. ☐

1 mark

33 Circle all the **prepositions** in the sentence below.

Before Mina tiptoed across the empty hallway, she peered cautiously through the gap in the door.

1 mark

34 Underline the **adverbial** in the sentence below.

When I said I didn't like football, Tomas looked at me as if I was mad.

1 mark

35 Circle the **subject** and underline the **object** in the sentence below.

The soldier stood on the castle battlements.

1 mark

36 Which of the sentences below contain a **relative clause**?

Tick **two.**

On Saturday, I went and helped Grandad in the garden. ☐

Grandad, whose garden is his pride and joy, is brilliant at growing roses. ☐

He also enjoys growing carrots, and last year his carrots won first prize in a competition. ☐

The garden, which is overshadowed by trees at one end, is a lovely place to play in. ☐

1 mark

37 Draw lines to show whether the **main clause** or the **subordinate clause** is underlined in each of the sentences below.

<u>I've never liked fishcakes</u>, because they don't really taste of anything.	main clause
<u>Digging about underneath the brambles and nettles</u>, Tamsin found a tiny door.	
On his first day at school, <u>Marek asked if he could sit at my table</u>.	subordinate clause
<u>When you open the present</u>, you'll get a big surprise!	

1 mark

38 Circle the two words that show the **tense** in the sentence below.

We went to the cinema on Saturday, but unfortunately the film was rubbish.

1 mark

39 Rewrite the sentence below so that it is in the **present tense**.

Dominic tried his very best, but he couldn't catch up with Malia.

____

1 mark

40

One of the verbs in the sentence below is in a different tense. Circle it, and write the correct form of the verb below.

Mattie woke with a start, leapt up from the bed and shoots downstairs to the front door.

1 mark

41

Rewrite the sentence below so that it is in the **passive voice**. Remember to punctuate your sentence correctly.

Maia's football broke most of the glass in the greenhouse.

1 mark

42 Add a **colon** in the correct place in this sentence.

I've had a brilliant idea I'm going to build my own space rocket.

1 mark

43 Complete the table by writing an **antonym** for each of the underlined words in the sentences below.

Word	Antonym
The blueberry ice-cream was absolutely delicious.	
I enjoy going shopping with Mum.	
When Marco opened the curtains, he could see it was going to be a chilly day.	
Dylan is the most helpful boy in the class.	

1 mark

44

Explain how the different hyphens change the **meanings** of the two sentences below

The pet shop has five year-old rabbits.

This means that ...

____

____

The pet shop has five-year-old rabbits.

This means that ...

____

____

1 mark

45 Which sentence uses the **short dash** correctly?

Tick **one**.

We all enjoyed the holiday even Daniel – who got stung by a wasp. ☐

We all enjoyed the holiday – even Daniel, who got stung by a wasp. ☐

We all enjoyed the holiday even Daniel, who got stung by a – wasp. ☐

We all enjoyed the holiday even – Daniel, who got stung by a wasp. ☐

1 mark

46 Insert one **semi-colon** in the correct place in this sentence.

We're going to have salad for tea it's far too hot to have soup.

1 mark

47 Add appropriate **suffixes** to turn the root words below into **adjectives**.

help____________________

comfort____________________

peace____________________

care____________________

1 mark

48

Add **commas** to the sentence below to show that all the children got the treat.

The children who had been good all term got a special treat.

1 mark

49

Rewrite the sentence below using **apostrophes** where they are needed.

The womens changing room wasnt in use that day, because there were decorators ladders and paint pots everywhere.

____

____

1 mark

Grammar, punctuation and spelling: spelling

Instructions

This booklet is for writing answers to the spelling test.

The test will take approximately **15 minutes**.

You will be read **20 sentences**.

Each sentence written in this booklet has a word missing.

Listen carefully to the missing word and write it in the gap.

Make sure you spell the missing word correctly.

Spelling

1. Dad cooked a very ______________________ meal.

2. Gran's dog has a ______________________ blanket to sleep on.

3. I would like to ask your ______________________ about something.

4. The ______________________ was full of people enjoying their meal.

5. Our rabbits had ______________________ babies.

6. I like doing ______________________, but I'm not very good at cartwheels.

7. The ______________________ put plenty of pepper in the stew.

8. Sasha is two years ______________________ than me.

9. Grandad fell asleep in front of the ______________________.

10. At the castle we saw some ______________________ jousting.

11. "I'll look after you," said Jack ______________________.

12. Mum gave Stefan a very ______________________ job.

13. Rob is eighteen, but he is rather ______________________.

14. Let me show you my most ______________________ possession.

15. Sam said he could swim, but that was an ______________________.

16. The ______________________ sang beautifully.

17. Aneeta ______________________ cleared the table.

18. It hurt when I bit my ______________________.

19. Dad has a nasty ______________________ today.

20. Text messages are a quick method of ______________________.

Answers: Reading Checkpoint Challenge

Poetry

1. The Garden is changing its clothes (1 mark)

2. dark, dull, drab (1 mark)

3. Answers may vary. Examples:
1) getting dressed/dressing up/putting on nice clothes
2) dancing (in the sun) (1 mark)

4. Answers may vary. Correct answers must include reference to different moods of winter and spring. Example: The author prefers spring because the garden is full of bright, happy colours (pink, white, green, purple) compared to winter when the colours are dull and dark (brown). (2 marks; award 1 mark for describing the author's feelings about either season with reference to the text; award 2 marks for describing the author's feelings about winter and spring with reference to the text)

5. a fable (1 mark)

6. to show words that are spoken / direct speech (1 mark)

7. fliers → seagulls
crawlers → centipedes
borers → moles
hooters → owls
roarers → lions
gulpers → frogs (1 mark)

8. small, slow smile or small, slow head (1 mark)

9. metaphor (1 mark)

10 marks

Non-fiction

10. the pancreas (1 mark)

11. insulin → a hormone that allows glucose into cells
glucose → a type of sugar
hypoglycaemia → illness bought on by low blood glucose
diabetic → someone with diabetes
carbohydrate → a type of food that contains sugars and starches (1 mark)

12. Answers may vary. Examples: by eating a healthy diet; by exercising. An acceptable answer could also include the results or examples of such measures (e.g. controlling glucose levels, diet, being fit, avoiding sweets) but not daily management procedures (blood testing, insulin injections, emergency glucose boosts). (1 mark)

Answers: Reading Checkpoint Challenge

13. Answers may vary. Example: The drink must contain sugar to give a glucose boost; diet drinks don't contain sugar. (1 mark)

14. Carbohydrates: rice, bread; Fruit and vegetables: broccoli, peach; Protein: salmon, chicken breast; Dairy products: cheese, yoghurt (1 mark)

15. Answers may vary. Example: ...they need to have enough glucose in their blood to last the night. (1 mark)

16. (an organ in your body) (1 mark)

17. a lancet, a test strip, a blood glucose meter (1 mark)

18. Facts: The hormone insulin helps your body use glucose for energy. A blood glucose level below 4 might indicate hypoglycaemia. Opinions: An insulin injection feels no worse than a pin prick. Anyone with diabetes can become an elite athlete. (1 mark)

19. Answers may vary. Example: If you inject yourself in the same place, then that area may get sore. (1 mark)

20. Emotional symptoms: irritated, confused, anxious; Physical symptom: sick, shaky, sweaty, cold. (1 mark)

21. a) Answers may vary. Example: it is important for them to have the right level of insulin in their bodies to be able to process the glucose about to come from their food. (2 marks; award 1 mark for a correct answer, 2 marks for a correct answer which uses evidence from the text to support it)

b) Answers may vary. Example: The insulin will start working too early and reduce the person's blood glucose level, which may trigger a hypoglycaemia attack. (2 marks; award 1 mark for a short correct answer, for example: the insulin will start working too early, 2 marks for a correct answer supported by evidence from the text)

15 marks

Fiction

22. 2, 4, 5, 3, 1, 6 (1 mark)

23. a) Answers may vary. Examples: a ghost/phantom/spirit
b) plenty (in this context, not a reward) (2 marks; award 1 mark for correctly answering part a, 1 mark for correctly answering part b)

24. (His horses' eyes glowed) as red as hot coals
(The air hissed dangerously) like a thousand cats. (1 mark)

25. She eats something (the six pomegranate seeds). (1 mark)

Answers: Reading Checkpoint Challenge

26. Answers may vary. Examples: his dark, billowing cloak; his dread gaze; his cold veins; his sour heart; the ghastly dark shadow. Answers must not include verbs and must include more than one noun on its own. For example, do not accept: 'his dark billowing cloak blotted out the sun' or just 'cloak' on its own. (1 mark)

27. antonyms (1 mark)

28. Demeter was crying too. (1 mark)

29. Answers may vary. Example: When Demeter is happy and proud the crops 'grow tall and healthy'. When she was 'filled with despair' the crops 'withered and rotted'. (2 marks; award 1 mark for an answer which references an effect one mood of Demeter's has on the crops, 2 marks for an answer which references the effect two different moods of Demeter have on the crops)

30. Answers may vary, but must use evidence from both the poem and story and contrast his quick temper in the poem with his level-headed fairness in the story. Example: In the poem, Zeus reacts angrily and cruelly. He 'roars' at the tortoise and gives it a punishment that lasts 'for evermore'. In the story, Zeus acts calmly and fairly by deciding that Persephone must split her time between 'the Underworld with Hades' and 'the upper world amongst the mortals' with her mother. (2 marks; only give 1 mark for an answer which does not refer to both texts, or does not make use of evidence from the texts. Give 2 marks for an answer which refers to both the poem and story, uses evidence from both and compares the different representations of Zeus.)

31. Answers may vary, but the answer must include the word 'seasons' (or a list of them) and evidence from the text linking the timings and conditions to the names of the seasons. Example: It explains the existence of the seasons. It mentions 'half a year' the world is 'cold and bare', which would be autumn and winter. It also says for 'six months ... life blossoms and blooms', which is spring and summer. (2 marks; award 1 mark for an answer which contains the word seasons and uses brief evidence from the text, 2 marks for a detailed answer which uses more evidence from the text to link the timings and conditions to the names of the seasons)

32. Answers may vary. Example: How the world got its seasons. (1 mark)

15 marks

TOTAL: 40 marks

MARK SCHEME: WRITING CHECKPOINT CHALLENGE

To achieve the standards detailed below, students should demonstrate attainment of each statement within this framework. All skills should be demonstrated before moving onto the next standard.

Some statements contain qualifiers (*some* and *most*). In this case, *most* indicates that the statement is generally met with occasional errors and *some* indicates that a skill is demonstrated correctly on occasion, but not consistently.

Tick each box when a skill is achieved to record individual student progress. Word lists for Years 3-4 and 5-6 can be accessed on the government website.

End of Key Stage 2 statutory assessment – Working towards the expected standard					
The student can write for a range of purposes and audiences:		**Fable**	**Diary**	**Persuasive writing**	**Explain**
• using paragraphs to organise ideas					
• describing settings and characters				N/A	N/A
• using some cohesive devices within and across sentences and paragraphs					
• using different verb forms (mostly accurately)					
• using co-ordinating and subordinating conjunctions					
• using (mostly correctly):	capital letters				
	full stops				
	question marks				
	exclamation marks				
	commas for lists				
	apostrophes for contraction				
• spelling most words from the Years 3 and 4 word list correctly					
• spelling some words from the Years 5 and 6 word list correctly					
• producing legible joined handwriting.					

MARK SCHEME: WRITING CHECKPOINT CHALLENGE

End of Key Stage 2 statutory assessment – Working at the expected standard					
The student can write for a range of purposes and audiences:		**Fable**	**Diary**	**Persuasive writing**	**Explain**
• creating atmosphere, and integrating dialogue to convey character and advance the action				N/A	N/A
• selecting vocabulary and grammatical structures that reflect the level of formality required (mostly correctly)					
• using a range of cohesive devices, including adverbials, within and across sentences and paragraphs					
• using passive and modal verbs appropriately					
• using a wide range of clause structures, sometimes varying their position within the					
• using adverbs, preposition phrases and expanded noun phrases effectively to add detail, qualification					
• using (mostly correctly):	inverted commas		N/A	N/A	N/A
	commas for clarity				
	punctuation for parenthesis				
• making some correct use of:	semi-colons				
	dashes				
	colons				
	hyphens				
• spelling most words from the Years 5 and 6 list correctly					
• maintaining legibility, fluency and speed in handwriting through choosing whether or not to join specific letters.					

MARK SCHEME: WRITING CHECKPOINT CHALLENGE

<table>
<tr><th colspan="6">End of Key Stage 2 statutory assessment – Working at greater depth within the expected standard</th></tr>
<tr><th colspan="2">The student can write for a range of purposes and audiences:</th><th>Fable</th><th>Diary</th><th>Persuasive writing</th><th>Explain</th></tr>
<tr><td colspan="2">• managing shifts between levels of formality through selecting vocabulary precisely and by manipulating grammatical structures</td><td></td><td></td><td></td><td></td></tr>
<tr><td colspan="2">• selecting verb forms for meaning and effect</td><td></td><td></td><td></td><td></td></tr>
<tr><td rowspan="2">• using the full range of punctuation taught at Key Stage 2, mostly correctly, including:</td><td>semi-colons to mark the boundary between independent clauses</td><td></td><td></td><td></td><td></td></tr>
<tr><td>colons to mark the boundary between independent clauses</td><td></td><td></td><td></td><td></td></tr>
</table>

Answers: Grammar and Punctuation Checkpoint Challenge

1. a pronoun (1 mark)

2. Oxford, Monday, I, Poland, January, Charles Darwin, Christmas (1 mark)

3. a) What a shame we didn't arrive on time!
b) Because it is an exclamation and the others are all questions. (1 mark)

4. "I've got a great idea," I said. "It's too hot, isn't it? Let's stop and get some ice-creams." (1 mark)

5. should've, won't, it's, you're, they're (1 mark)

6. began, ran, said, threw, won (1 mark)

7. younger, quick, nimble, older, strong, (very is an adverb) (1 mark)

8. Couldn't we all stop arguing and try to get along?
How delicious that milkshake was!
I read a comic every morning; I draw my own cartoons in the evening. (1 mark)

9. The living room window was shattered by a cricket ball.
The little girl's doll was run over by the enormous, noisy lorry. (1 mark)

10. [M]UST, M[A]Y, MI[G]HT, W[I]LL, [C]AN = MAGIC (1 mark)

11. moody → moodily; simple → simply; angry → angrily; good → well; fast → fast; (hard should not be joined to hardly) (1 mark)

12. Harriet ate a slice of pizza, two cartons of apple juice, an orange and a boiled egg for lunch.
Bravery, generosity, calmness under pressure and reliability are some of his characteristics. (1 mark)

Answers: Grammar and Punctuation Checkpoint Challenge

13. Prepositions showing time: since, until, at, ago, during
Prepositions showing position: near, over, through, above, across (1 mark)

14. your, its, their (1 mark)

15. I was surprised I enjoyed the white-water rafting (I usually avoided terrifying activities). (1 mark)

16. a) My dad always wears a thick jumper → even when it is baking hot.
Our dog Pip would bark madly → whenever someone knocked at the door.
I sometimes cheat at cards → although I would never admit it

b) Even when it is baking hot, my dad always wears a thick jumper.
Whenever someone knocked at the door, our dog Pip would bark madly.
Although I would never admit it, I sometimes cheat at cards. (1 mark)

17. Some, Other, The, a (1 mark)

18. In an emergency, do the following: exit your room, avoid using the lift and raise the alarm.
Our journey just got worse and worse: the car broke down in the rain. (1 mark)

19. has frozen, have destroyed, has captivated (1 mark)

20. the girl's chair, the children's toys, the wolves' howling, Thomas's basketballs (1 mark)

21. a) She runs very fast around the athletics track.

b) Because it is in the simple present tense; the other sentences are all in the future tense. (1 mark)

22. Tyler admitted that he still didn't know how to ride a bike.
My mum asked if I had remembered my PE kit. (1 mark)

23. barking → crazy; cheesed off → annoyed; geezer → man; jammy → lucky; minted → wealthy;
scarper → run away (1 mark)

Answers: Grammar and Punctuation Checkpoint Challenge

24. a pair of brackets, a pair of dashes, a pair of commas (1 mark)

25. My great uncle, who fought in the Korean War, celebrated his 90th birthday recently.
We are proud of our new cows, which came from a farm in Devon.
Sir Gwyn Broadsword, whose arms were short and whose hands were tiny, didn't enjoy fighting.
(1 mark)

26. The ex-footballer bought a sports car at an eye-watering price.
My sister-in-law likes to re-cover her armchairs with old-fashioned materials. (1 mark)

27. and, if, so, when, but (1 mark)

28. Bex loves to watch old movies; her friends prefer reality TV shows.
Camels are suited to life in the desert; they can go for days without water. (1 mark)

29. Early every morning, the milkman delivers his dairy products to our street.

The author was delighted by the latest reviews of his new book.

A stooping man, who was wearing a long coat, approached some tall gates uncertainly. (1 mark)

30. every morning, our street, his new book, a long coat (1 mark)

31. How? By helicopter; Where? At the crime scene; When? At the crack of dawn. (1 mark)

32. Didn't you know that we are going to Disneyland tomorrow?
Have you and Dad decided when to go shopping? (1 mark)

33. 1, 5, 6, 4, 2, 3 (1 mark)

34. Have you done the mowing yet? It looks as if it is about to rain.
Please write to your grandma. You don't want to hurt her feelings, do you? (1 mark)

ANSWERS: GRAMMAR AND PUNCTUATION CHECKPOINT CHALLENGE

35. Whenever Georgie felt sad, she went to visit her aunt, uncle and their tortoise Gerald.
Although Max's room was smelly, untidy and dusty, he thought it was just perfect.
Even if I agreed to watch you do it, I won't join in with the singing, dancing or acting. (1 mark)

36. past progressive (1 mark)

37. hyphen, single dash, hyphens (1 mark)

38. If you see the warning light, <u>stop</u> immediately and <u>call</u> for help.
When the dough has doubled in size, <u>remove</u> it from the bowl and <u>knock</u> out the air. (1 mark)

39. a long, shaggy-haired dog, my front door, its friendly, intelligent eyes, anyone with a dog, some fresh water. (1 mark)

40. a) They had eaten far too much pizza for lunch.
b) Because it is in the past perfect tense and the others are all in the present prefect tense. (1 mark)

TOTAL: 40 marks

ANSWERS: SPELLING CHECKPOINT CHALLENGE

1. inpossible (impossible) (1 mark)

2. horses, roofs (1 mark)

3. bought, thought (1 mark)

4. aggressive, temperature, government, forty (2 marks; award 1 mark for two correct spellings, 2 marks for four correct spellings)

5. necessary, persuade, parliament (1 mark)

6. **a)** two or too; **b)** hear; **c)** piece; **d)** break (2 marks; award 1 mark for two correct homophones, 2 marks for all four correct)

7. **a)** vis **b)** the ability to see (2 marks; award 1 mark for part a) and 1 mark for part b) answered correctly)

8. Across: 3. bruise, 6. amateur, 7. cemetery, 9. neighbor, 10. lightning
Down: 1. soldier, 2. queue, 4. shoulder, 5. restaurant, 8. yacht (5 marks; award 1 mark for two correct answers, 2 marks for four correct answers, 3 marks for six correct answers, 4 marks for eight correct answers, and 5 marks for ten correct answers)

9. different, rhyme, muscle, library, business, vegetable (hidden word: resist) (3 marks; award 1 mark for two correct spellings, 2 marks for four correct spellings, 3 marks for five correct spellings and finding the correct hidden word)

10. brave → cowardly, lowest → highest, quiet → loud, enemy → friend, true → false (2 marks; award 1 mark for correctly drawing lines from each word to its antonym, and another mark for correctly spelling all the antonyms)

ANSWERS: SPELLING CHECKPOINT CHALLENGE

11. +ance: assistance, clearance; +ence: correspondence, obedience, violence; +ible: accessible, reversible, collectible (3 marks; award 1 mark for correctly filling in one column of the table, 2 marks for correctly filling in two columns of the table, 3 marks for filling in the whole table correctly)

12. quite, except, affect, advise (2 marks; award 1 mark for two correct answers, 2 marks for four correct answers)

13. unhappy, inflexible, mislead, irreplaceable (2 marks; award 1 mark for two correct answers, 2 marks for four correct answers)

14. foreign, communicate, language, awkward, dictionary, appreciate (3 marks; award 1 mark for two underlined and correctly spelled words, 2 marks for four underlined and correctly spelled words, 3 marks for all six words underlined and correctly spelled)

15. ten inches, a bag full of potatoes, two halves, lots of crying babies (2 marks; award 1 mark for two correct answers, 2 marks for four correct)

16. unhappy, difficulty, nervous, pricey, courteous (4 marks; award 1 mark for two correct spellings, 2 marks for three correct spellings, 3 marks for four correct spellings, 4 marks for five correct spellings)

17. field, diesel, seize (1 mark)

18. physical, secretary, achievement, embarrassed (2 marks; award 1 mark for two correct spellings, 2 marks for four correct spellings)

19. ambicious (ambitious) (1 mark)

TOTAL: 40 marks

Answers: Topic Tests

1 Diagnostic
Not applicable

2 Question types
1. she always gave me a packet of sweets (1 mark)
2. I will never go jogging at night. → future, I would never go jogging at night. → modal, I never go jogging at night. → simple present (1 mark)
3. expanded noun phrase (1 mark)
4. It's a busy time of year: most of our visitors arrive in August. (2 marks; 1 mark for each correct use of punctuation)
5. true, false, false, false (2 marks; 1 mark for two correct answers, 2 marks for four correct answers)
6. friendly faces, sizzling sausages, warm welcome (3 marks; 1 mark for each correct alliterative phrase)

3 Non-fiction features
1. autobiography, science investigation, diary entry, encyclopaedia page, product instructions (3 marks; 1 mark for two correct answers, 2 marks for four correct answers, 3 marks for all five correct answers)
2. a title starting with 'how', technical vocabulary (1 mark)
3. an eye-catching headline, different points of view (1 mark)
4. Standard English, the writer's address (1 mark)
5. Should the police have guns? → a balanced argument, How to make the most of your stay in Florida → an information leaflet, Barry Snotter and the brilliant show! → a theatre review, Olympic crisps, top of the podium → a magazine advert (2 marks; 1 mark for two correct lines, 2 marks for four correct lines)
6. Answers may vary. Examples: (question as) title, sub-headings, paragraphs, introduction, points for, points against, conclusion, conjunctions (2 marks; 1 mark for two correct features, 2 marks for four correct features)

4 Finding answers
1. Moon, Mission, miles, module (2 marks)
2. **a)** Apollo 13 **b)** April 13th 1970 **c)** Jack Swigert **d)** 300,000 miles **e)** Houston (1 mark)
3. Ingenuity (1 mark)
4. Answers may vary. Example: An exploding fuel tank caused a loss of power and oxygen. (2 marks)

5 Character, theme and language
1. character → someone in a story, a person's personality and appearance, theme → a pattern of ideas or a related sequence of events, setting → where a story takes place, plot → the events that make up a story (2 marks; 1 mark for each two definitions)
2. **a)** unconfident, **b)** positive (allow annoying), **c)** proud (allow smart) (3 marks)
3. Answers may vary. Example: The theme of the story is Sunil's good luck. (1 mark)
4. Answers may vary, but must create the desired mood. Examples: **a)** The wind whispered gently through the trees. (calm) **b)** Harris stormed out of the room and slammed the door violently. (angry) **c)** "I can't wait to go!" shouted Vicki happily. (sad) **d)** The strange, wooden door swung open with a long creak. (mysterious) (4 marks)

6 Meaning
1. **a)** some rubbish **b)** a group **c)** absorbent material **d)** a covered chair on poles (4 marks)
2. Answers may vary. Examples: **a)** huge / enormous **b)** pretty **c)** awful **d)** wealthy (2 marks)
3. inferring (1 mark)
4. Answers may vary. Example: Saying what will happen next / in the future (1 mark)
5. the events so far, the behaviour of the characters (2 marks)

7 Making comparisons and summarising
1. Answers may vary, but should contrast George's shyness with his brother's confidence (2 marks). Award 2 further marks for textual evidence for these traits. Example: George is shy. He is nervous of 'all those eyes staring at him' and 'his hand is shaking'.

Answers: Topic Tests

2. Answers may vary, but should detail how George moves from fear to anger / embarrassment. Example: At first, George is scared of making his speech. When his brother takes over, he becomes cross and embarrassed. He messes up his speech, scowls and his cheeks go red. (2 marks)
3. a statement of the main message or idea, a brief version of the plot (2 marks)
4. Answers may vary. Example: Shy George fails to give a speech so his confident bother takes over instead, leaving George feeling humiliated. (2 marks)

8 Poetry (similes and metaphors)

1. Similes: I slept like a log. She laughs like a hyena.
   My teacher is as wise as an owl. Metaphors: The sea was a mirror. At sunset, the clouds were pink cotton wool. You are my sunshine. (3 marks; award 1 mark per two correct answers)
2. **b)** [The forest fire] devoured the landscape like [a beast from a fiery underworld]. **c)** [The supporters of that politician] are [puppets on a string]. **d)** [That invention of yours] is as much use as [a chocolate teapot]. (2 marks)
3. Across: 3. knife; 5. umbrella
   Down: 1. song; 2. desert; 4. camel
4. **a)** I'm as thirsty as a camel in the desert. **b)** The tree was a wonderful, green umbrella. **c)** The wind in the trees was like a sad song. **d)** The moon was a curved, silver knife. (5 marks)

9 Poetry (other figurative language)

1. personification → a word that gives a non-human thing human characteristics, alliteration → a series of words beginning with the same letter, onomatopoeia → a word that copies the sound of the thing it is describing (1 mark)
2. cunning countess, crimson couch, counted coins carefully (1 mark)
3. cracked, rumbled (1 mark)
4. danced (1 mark)
5. **a)** rustled [O: Onomatopoeia]; **b)** didn't [A: alliteration]; **c)** sneaked [P: personification] (3 marks)
6. **b)** AO: alliteration (wild wind), onomatopoeia (bang) **c)** PAO: personification (dragged), alliteration (smell of sizzling sausages), onomatopoeia (sizzling) **d)** PO: personification (screamed), onomatopoeia (popped) (3 marks; award 1 each for correct answers to parts b, c and d)

10 Audience and purpose

1. Answers may vary. Example: who you are writing for (1 mark)
2. Answers may vary. Examples: why you are writing / the point of the writing / what you are trying to say. (1 mark)
3. food advert → to persuade, a visitor's guide → to inform, a bike maintenance manual → to instruct (3 marks)
4. Answers may vary. Examples: rhyming words, repeated words, funny words, repeated structure. Do not accept visual features, such as illustrations or large text. (2 marks)
5. Answers may vary. Example: Audience: mums or dads with young children / toddlers. Purpose: to instruct (also accept to inform). Evidence: 'your little angel' is evidence for the audience, bossy (imperative) verbs, such as 'keep', 'fit' and 'move' are evidence for the purpose. (3 marks; 1 mark each for audience, purpose and evidence)

11 The writing process

1. writing 3, organising 2, editing 4, proof-reading 5, planning 1 (1 mark)
2. **a)** Be clear on the audience and purpose **b)** Write your ideas down quickly **c)** Organise your ideas (3 marks)
3. Answers should include reference to a collection of sentences and to the idea that the sentences are about the same subject. Example: A paragraph is a group of sentences that are about the same thing. (2 marks)
4. Conjunctions (1 mark)
5. **b)** Don't **c)** Do **d)** Don't **e)** Don't **f)** Don't **g)** Do (3 marks)

12 The editing process

1. Answers may vary. Examples: **a)** Nick ate bacon and eggs with toast and jam for breakfast every day. (word order change for clarity) **b)** My boss is a kind person. (removal of double negative) **c)** Lauren enjoys reading and writing. (passive to active) (3 marks)
2. Answers may vary, but should include two of the following: Does it suit the audience and purpose? Is it organised into paragraphs? Have I repeated myself or missed any points out? Have I written clearly? (2 marks)

Answers: Topic tests

3. Putting on a suit of armour was a difficult task. It normally required the help of another person. First the knight's squire helped the knight into his padded tunic. This had pieces of chain mail sewn into it at the danger spots. It also had a number of laces, which were used to tie on pieces of armour. Once the armour was attached, the last things to be put on were the gauntlets and helmet. (5 marks; 1 mark per two corrections)

13 Writing articles

1. Answers may vary, but should include reference to print and digital media. Example: in a newspaper; on a website. (2 marks)
2. give both sides of a story. (1 mark)
3. facts and opinions. (1 mark)
4. Answers may vary. Examples: headline, byline, paragraphs, quotations, photographs (2 marks)
5. Answer may vary. Award marks for use of alliteration and brevity. Examples: Headline: Jack and Jill in hill kill. Subheading: Mystery of broken bucket
Headline: Spider spooks tuffet toddler. Subheading: Alarming arachnid still at large (4 marks)

14 Writing explanations

1. how, why (1 mark)
2. in time order / in the order things happen (1 mark)
3. Time links: next, finally, when, until; Causal links: so, therefore, as a result, because, in this way (5 marks)
4. Simple present (1 mark)
5. Answers may vary. Examples: A smartphone is an interactive communication device that allows you to talk to other people and access information from the internet.
A games console is an electronic device use to play games on a TV screen to which it is connected. (2 marks)

15 Persuasive letters

1. **a)** your / my address **b)** top right (2 marks)
2. Answers may vary, but must include a salutation with a title and name and a salutation to an unnamed person.
Examples: **a)** Dear Mr Moore, Dear Mrs Jones, Dear Ms Robinson, Dear Miss Patel **b)** Dear Sir or Madam, Dear Sir, Dear Madam (2 marks)
3. Answer may vary. Example: regarding, with reference to, what the letter is about, in the matter of, subject of the letter, subject line (1 mark)
4. Answers may vary. Examples: I feel that; You must agree that; In my opinion; Surely. (2 marks)
5. What you / I hope will happen next. (1 mark)
6. When you know the person (1 mark)
7. When you don't know the person (1 mark)

16 Balanced arguments

1. Answers may vary. Example: both points of view / both sides of the argument / point for and against (1 mark)
2. introduction 2, title (question) 1, points against 4, points for 3, conclusion 5 (1 mark)
3. Answers may vary. Examples include: less pollution; reduction in related health problems; fewer traffic jams; more relaxing / fewer stressed drivers; easier for buses, deliveries and emergency vehicles to move around; delays cost people and businesses money; fewer accidents (4 marks)
4. Answers may vary. Example: Should circuses use animal acts? (1 mark)
5. firstly, in addition, for example, consequently (2 marks, 1 mark per two correct answers)
6. (my / your) own opinion (1 mark)

ANSWERS: TOPIC TESTS

17 Writing fiction

1. a) first person, past tense **b)** third person, present tense **c)** third person, past tense (3 marks)
2. Answers may vary. Ensure past tense verb and first person voice has been used. (1 mark)
3. solution 4, opening 1, build-up 2, ending 5, problem 3 (1 mark)
4. the main characters, the setting, the mood (3 marks; 1 mark per two correct answers)
5. Answers may vary. One mark should be awarded for each sentence that includes both physical and personality characteristics. (2 marks)

18 Nouns

1. Common nouns: friends, sadness, women, breakfast, journeys. Proper nouns: Easter, January, Newcastle, Emily, Tuesday (5 marks; 1 mark per two correct answers)
2. b) the park, his way **c)** the bottom of the hotel pool, a thick layer of green slime; **d)** everybody the family, an enormous chocolate birthday cake (3 marks)
3. Answers may vary. Example: Every cute, little pet needs a nice, friendly owner. (2 marks)

19 Pronouns and determiners

1. b) Layla and I found some sweets. We ate all of them.
c) Paloma was upset with me and Annabel. Actually, she was really cross with us. (2 marks)
2. an, some, the, those, your, another, two, all, its, no (5 marks; 1 mark per two correct answers)
3. Your aunt Carolyn lives on her farm in Wales. My uncle George works on his farm next to hers. The farm next to that isn't theirs: it's ours! (1 mark)
4. a) ours, theirs **b)** your, mine (2 marks)

20 Adjectives and adverbs

1. Across: 4. unfortunate, 5. weak, 6. most, 8. irregular, 9. heaviest.
Down: 1. older, 2. interesting, 3. narrowest, 7. worst, 8. slower (4 marks; 1 mark per two correct answers)
2. a) The fat cat stretched lazily on the carpet.; **b)** Lee, a thin builder, drove to work quickly and worked non-stop.; **c)** When I was younger, it was really exciting to go to the circus. ; **d)** Mina got up very slowly and put on her crumpled red t-shirt. (4 marks)
3. a) Fifty years from now, there may be humans living on Mars. In the future, who knows how far we will travel?
b) After all the long speeches, Jodie was really thirsty. At the bar, she ordered a pint of water with ice and lemon. (2 marks)

21 Verbs – present

1. Simple present: it goes; I find; Present progressive: I am running; it is getting; Present perfect: I have reached; a spider has spun (3 marks)
2. b) A dog has chased me and now it has licked me. **c)** He has drunk too many fizzy drinks and his teeth have fallen out. **d)** My family and I have often visited France but we have never flown. (3 marks)
3. b) Have you seen that new sci-fi film? **c)** He is becoming even more powerful! **d)** I have spoken to your teacher. **e)** They are beginning to understand. (4 marks)

22 Verbs – past

1. was breaking; shook; were thrown; lasted; was killed; were left (3 marks; 1 mark per two correct answers)
2. The tap was leaking. → past progressive; I took the last bus home. → simple past; Connor had never seen a pantomime→ past perfect (1 mark)
3. b) Dad took our dog to the vets. **c)** My uncles always forgot my birthday. **d)** The priest lit the candles. (3 marks)
4. travelled, were, loved, caught, explored, didn't (3 marks; 1 mark for each two correct answers)

23 Verbs – future and modal

1. b) past; **c)** future; **d)** future; **e)** past; **f)** future; **g)** present (3 marks; 1 mark for each two correct answers)
2. Would (1 mark)
3. Answers may vary. Examples: Future: will rise, is going to flood, will have to run, will cut off, will be plunged, is going to be
Modal: might rise, could flood, may have to run, might cut off, would be plunged, would be (6 marks; 1 mark for each correct verb in the future and modal tense)

ANSWERS: TOPIC TESTS

24 Conjunctions and prepositions

1. Co-ordinating conjunctions: nor, but, so yet,or; Subordinating conjunctions: because, until, whenever, although, unless (2 marks; 1 for each correctly filled in column)

2. from, down, under, through, onto, behind, between, across, after, towards (2 marks)

3. Answers may vary. Examples: **b)** My little brother hides under the table whenever it's time for bed. **c)** Although she's over 90, Lola's granny walked from London to Paris. **d)** The teacher is always firm but fair towards everyone in the class. (6 marks)

25 Sentence types

1. b) Q: question **c)** C: command **d)** S: statement **e)** E: exclamation (2 marks; 1 mark per two correct answers)

2. b) It is time to water the garden, isn't it? **c)** We were supposed to meet at the swimming pool, weren't we? (1 mark for two correct answers)

3. a) Empty the bottle and fill it with fresh water. **b)** When you hear the whistle, be quick and run towards the house. (1 mark for two correct answers)

4. "Hurry up!" shouted Dad. "You don't want to miss the start, do you?" I charged downstairs and sprinted to the car. What was the time? I glanced at my watch. We only had minutes to get there. "Have you got everything?" my mum asked. I nodded. Dad turned the key. Nothing happened. Dad shook his head and said, "What a time for this to happen!" (6 marks; 1 mark for two correct uses of punctuation, 2 marks for four correct uses, 3 marks for five correct, 4 marks for 6 correct, etc.)

26 Subject and object

1. b) my grandmother and I **c)** it (1 mark)

2. b) all his money **c)** a group of monkeys (1 mark)

3. a) The wolf howled at the moon. **b)** I was taught to play rounders by Mr Clark. **c)** The rising tide could have washed us away. **d)** A crying baby completely ruined the movie. (4 marks)

4. a) stadium (S); destroyed (V); storm (O) **b)** car (s) stolen (V) (2 marks)

5. b) was eaten; **c)** was given; **d)** was ridden; **e)** was thrown (2 marks)

27 Clauses

1. b) Four months earlier, just before summer, the Watsons had arrived in New York. **c)** Vincent Starlight, who was an ageing rock star, couldn't find his electric guitar. (2 marks)

2. b) Jerôme, who comes from Brittany in France, is staying with us for a few days. **c)** While she was chasing a cat, my puppy fell into the pond. (2 marks)

3. b) We will never get tickets for the Olympics unless we book early. **c)** Whenever the birds start singing, I always get woken up early. **d)** Meg twisted her ankle on a walk when she was on holiday in Spain. (3 marks)

4. b) The farmer, whose sheep had disappeared, was sad and confused. My friend Patrick, who once ate ten sausages, is going to America. The parcel that was supposed to arrive today has gone missing. (3 marks)

28 Standard English

1. Yours sincerely, I would be grateful, In reference to your letter, In my opinion (2 marks; 1 mark for each two correct answers)

2. b) non-Standard English **c)** Standard English **d)** Standard English **e)** non-Standard English (2 marks)

3. Yesterday, Ben and I were so bored that we went to town. I saw some trainers that looked like a good deal but I didn't have any money because I'd run out. I phoned my mum. She said I should have saved up. I wasn't happy. (6 marks; 1 mark per 2 correct changes to Standard English)

29 Basic sentence punctuation

1. ?.! (1 mark)

2. b) The pack of dogs barked. **c)** Eventually the sun disappeared. **d)** All the delicious, creamy ice-creams were melting. (3 marks)

3. Answers may vary. Examples: **b)** Why don't we go to the cinema on Friday? **c)** What an amazing experience that was! **d)** It's not fair! How is it I always get the blame? (3 marks)

Answers: Topic Tests

4. "Dad, have you remembered that it's my birthday soon?" I asked. Dad sighed. "How could I forget? You remind me every other day."
"Well, I was hoping you'd buy me some new boots," I said hopefully. "How much are they, darling?" asked Mum.
I hesitated and replied, "Only two hundred pounds."
"What?" roared Dad. "Are you insane?" (3 marks; 1 mark per 6 correct uses of punctuation)

30 Commas

1. b) While it was pouring with rain, we played in the mud for hours. **c)** Whenever I'm really hungry, I eat a whole bunch of bananas. **d)** Unless you can persuade me otherwise, I'm going to do it. (3 marks)
2. b) Fred, Tom, Joe, Alistair and Amir are all coming to my party tomorrow. **c)** Eliza, who is tall, thin and generous, loves to exercise, read and swim. (2 marks)
3. Although Sara, Maisie and Taya enjoyed netball, they preferred playing basketball. (1 mark)
4. Just as Cameron was falling asleep, there was a strange noise. He sat up sharply, peered around the dark room, listened carefully and then wondered if he had imagined it. He flopped back but then he heard it again. Although he didn't want to admit it, it was clear someone else was in his room. (4 marks)

31 Parenthesis

1. A pair of brackets can be used for parenthesis (just like in this sentence). (1 mark)
2. b) Many people, especially people who are old, struggle to use computers. **c)** My cousin, whose friend is a movie star, is taking me to a film premiere. **d)** Gordon, who is an experienced mountaineer, climbed to the summit in record time. **e)** An old sports car, which made an incredible noise, was on show at the fair. (4 marks)
3, 4. Answers may vary. Examples: **a)** Sir Francis Drake (1540–1596) was a famous Tudor sea captain. **b)** The opera, which I was forced to watch, was long and boring. **c)** The Nile Crocodile (Crocodylus niloticus) can grow up to 6 metres long. **d)** The stranger, a short man with dark hair and a cold, was listening to our conversation. **e)** My uncle – the one with the extra toe – can't wear ordinary shoes. (5 marks; 1 mark for each correctly drawn line and rewritten sentence)

32 Colons and semi-colons

1. a) I am hungry: I haven't eaten anything since breakfast. **b)** Lula got what she wanted: her mum gave her a fluffy scarf for winter. (2 marks)
2. a) Send me a text tomorrow; I'll let you know where we are meeting up. **b)** When we play rugby, I love chasing and tackling; you prefer dodging and kicking. (2 marks)
3. b) Marco loved cooked breakfasts: sausages, beans, a fried egg and bacon. **c)** The following items are for sale: a cot, some blankets, cuddly toys and a pram. **d)** On holiday in Greece we visited: a canyon in Crete called the Samaria Gorge; the ancient theatre of Delphi; and the Parthenon on top of the Acropolis in Athens. **e)** At the Chinese restaurant, I ordered: a bowl of delicious sweet and sour pork; a plate of vegetable dumplings; stir-fried chicken noodles; and Peking duck in pancakes. (6 marks; 1 mark each for parts b and c, two marks each for parts d and e)

33 Apostrophes

1. Boris's birthday; the women's shoes; the boys' headphones; the ducks' quacking; the children's toys (3 marks; 1 mark for two correct answers, 2 marks for four correct answers, 3 marks for all five correct answers)
2. 1) I am; **2)** who is; **3)** was not; **4)** it is; **5)** we are; **6)** does not; **7)** she had; **8)** we have (4 marks; 1 mark per two correct answers)
3. b) I should've taken Yasmin's things to her earlier. **c)** Why's it always your brother's turn on the console? **d)** It'll be soon be too late to save Mike's lost animals. (3 marks)

34 Punctuating speech

1. b) Brendan whispered, "You will never get away with this!" **c)** "Why don't you buy a new one?" asked my friend. **d)** "We are not too late. There is still time!" urged Katie. (3 marks)
2. a) "You could start a new hobby," suggested my mum.
b) Talvinder said, "Isn't it great? The holidays start tomorrow." (2 marks)

Answers: Topic tests

3. Thomas asked how long it would take to get there.
"It will take at least three hours," I told him.
He moaned that he was bored already.
"You should read your book or play on your phone,"
I suggested.
He reminded me that he got carsick if he did that.
(5 marks; 1 mark per correctly changed sentence)

35 Hyphens and single dashes

1. a) and **b)** Hyphen: Do you want a full-time or a part-time job? Single dash: The film was fantastic – but then I like anything! Hyphen and single dash: My father-in-law seems nice – or is he? (2 marks; 1 mark for two correct sentences, 2 marks for three correct sentences)

2. a little-known fact; a man-eating tiger; a twenty-storey building; an English-speaking country; a last-minute warning; a long-lasting friendship; a mouth-watering choice of puddings; a thought-provoking documentary. (4 marks; 1 mark per two correct answers)

3. a) My twelve-year-old son is really funny – at least, I think so! **b)** My instructor said I'll need self-discipline to re-educate my body and mind. **c)** Dad is going to be forty-two next week – sorry, I mean forty-three. (3 marks)

36 Word families

1. form (1 mark)

2. b) illogical **c)** impatient **d)** misspell **e)** unknown (2 marks; 1 mark per two correct answers)

3. b) educational **c)** fantastic;**d)** sensible **e)** ambitious (2 marks; 1 mark per each two correct answers)

4. pianos, alleys, women, children, babies, chefs, knives, strawberries, kangaroos, roofs (5 marks; 1 mark for each two correct answers)

37 Synonyms, antonyms and homophones

1. Synonyms: solid /study, temple / shrine. Antonyms: correct / wrong, joy / sadness. Homophones: plane / plain, brake / break (3 marks)

2. b) hear **c)** whether **d)** two, too **e)** their, they're (3 marks; 1 mark for two correct answers, 2 marks for three correct, 3 marks for four correct answers)

3. Across: 3. peace, 5. allowed, 7. different, 9. adults, 10. which.
Down: 1. greedy, 2. soldier, 4. lead, 6. wealthy, 8. injury (4 marks; 1 mark for four correct, 2 marks for six correct, 3 marks for eight correct, 4 marks for ten correct)

38 Tricky spellings

1. a) psychic, weird, thorough, believe **b)** ghost, different, average, Wednesday (2 marks)

2. b) knives **c)** achievement **d)** interested **e)** environment (2 marks; 1 mark per two correct answers)

3. fierce (1 mark)

4. Across: 4. knight, 5. library, 7. muscle, 9. vegetable, 10. plough. Down: 1. dough, 2. field, 3. diesel, 6. believe, 8. Ceiling (5 marks; 1 mark per two correct answers)

Mark scheme: Reading practice paper

This table shows you how marks are awarded for each of the questions in the reading test. The references in the 'Questions' column (2a, 2d etc.) show you which aspects of the Content Domain are covered by each question.

Some of the questions in the reading test are 'open', and require the student to use inference or give their own opinion. Example answers have been given to help you decide whether to award the mark or not, but bear in mind that different students may approach these questions in different ways. As a general rule, if a student's answer makes sense in the context of the text, and if (when asked to) they have used evidence from the text to support their answer convincingly, then their answer is acceptable. In the reading test, it is important to consider the content of a student's answer, and mistakes in grammar, spelling and presentation should not prevent the awarding of the mark as long as the student's meaning is clear and the content of the answer is correct.

Section 1: Jellyfish – mark scheme

Question	Requirement	Mark
1. 2b	Award **one** mark for ticking the correct option. Jellyfish can grow much bigger than most plankton. ☑	**1**
2. 2b	Award **two** marks for any two of: *jellyfish are wobbly, a bit like jelly; jellyfish are mostly made of water, like jelly; jellyfish contain protein, like jelly; some jellyfish can be eaten, like jelly.*	**2**
3. 2b	Award **one** mark for circling the correct option: its oral arms	**1**
4. 2d	Award **one** mark for a reasonable opinion about the author's likely views on eating jellyfish. Award **one** mark for backing up this opinion with quoted evidence. For example: *I think the author doesn't like the idea of eating jellyfish, because s/he describes them as 'slimy', and s/he says 'You may not be keen on the idea of tucking into a plateful of jellyfish and chips'*; or *I think the author does like the idea of eating jellyfish, because s/he says 'in some places around the world, people do enjoy eating jellyfish', and says that jellyfish can be turned into 'tasty meals', and that eating jellyfish might be necessary for more people in the future.*	**2**
5. 2b	Award **one** mark for ticking the correct option. it doesn't have one ☑	**1**
6. 2a	Award **one** mark for circling the correct phrase: sends the jellyfish forward	**1**

7. 2f	Award **one** mark for each of two sensible reasons why a diagram is included in the text. For example: *to convey detailed information that can't easily be shown in words alone; to show that a jellyfish is more complicated than edible jelly; because it is not easy to work out which part of a jellyfish is which just by looking at it; to help with understanding the explanation about how jellyfish move.*	**2**
8. 2a	Award **one** mark for the answer '*slimy*'.	**1**
9. 2c	Award **one** mark for a subheading that sums up the main idea. For example: *People can eat jellyfish* or *Food of the future?*	**1**
10. 2a	Award **one** mark for ticking the correct option. treat ☑	**1**
11. 2d	Award **one** mark for an explanation based on the information in the text and diagram. For example, *The jellyfish moves its hollow body in the water and this movement makes the water shoot out through the body cavity. The movement of the water makes the jellyfish move forwards.*	**1**
12. 2g	Award **one** mark for 'a plague of slimy Nomura jellyfish nearly two metres wide'.	**1**

12 questions, 15 marks

SECTION 2: THE HERON'S FEATHER – MARK SCHEME

Question	Requirement	Mark
13. 2b	Award **one** mark for ticking the correct option. boring ☑	**1**
14. 2g	**a)** Award **one** mark for a sensible explanation that accords with the text. For example: *The author wanted to get the reader's attention at the start of the story by suggesting that something strange and interesting has happened.* **b)** Award **one** mark for the student expressing their opinion in a reasonable way and in keeping with the text. For example: *Yes, I think it is effective, because it sounds as though Casey is really talking to the reader and it made me want to read on to find out what she had seen.*	**2**
15. 2b	Award **one** mark for circling the correct option. because it was quite cheap	**1**

16. 2b	Award **one** mark for ticking the two correct options. cooking on a campfire ☑ settling down for the night in the tent ☑	**1**
17. 2d 2f	Award **two** marks for an answer that shows the student understands that the author has planted the information about the Bronze Age burial site early in the story so that later, the reader will realise the boy Casey sees is probably from the Bronze Age and in some way connected with the burial site.	**2**
18. 2a 2b	Award **one** mark for the correct word: snoring.	**1**
19. 2d 2f	Award **one** mark, up to a total of **three**, for an appropriate description of Casey's feelings, together with evidence from the text, at each of the three required points. For example: *When she first saw the campsite... Casey felt as though she wasn't going to have much fun*. Evidence: *She mentions that there was no Wi-Fi, no one to play with, no shower etc., and she says 'There's nothing around us but woods and fields', and 'At first I thought it was going to be really boring'. When she was watching the huge bird in flight ... Casey felt in awe of how beautiful it was.* Evidence: *She says 'it soared away like the most graceful creature in the world,' and she watched it until it disappeared. When she first saw the strange boy ... Casey was alarmed because he looked so odd, and she thought he might be going to throw his spear at her.* Evidence: *She says 'At first I thought he was a girl,' and 'He had a long spear in one hand, and for a moment I thought he was going to throw it at me.'*	**3**
20. 2d	Award **one** mark for an answer that shows the student has understood that the boy is probably a young Bronze Age hunter rather than a modern child. Award **one more** mark for at least one piece of relevant evidence from the text. For example: the boy's clothes, the fact that he is carrying a spear, the unusual/old-fashioned way that he talks in the final paragraph.	**2**
21. 2b 2d	Award **one** mark for an answer that shows Casey in the field where her tent is, at the end of the field near the stream, and the boy on the other bank of the stream opposite her.	**1**
22. 2a	Award **one** mark for ticking the correct option. a building of historical importance ☑	**1**
23. 2c	Award **one** mark for a title that sums up the main theme or message of the story. For example: 'Casey and the Strange Boy', or 'Meeting Across the Years', or 'A Strange Meeting'.	**1**

24. 2d 2a 2f	**a)** Award **one** mark for an answer that shows the student understands italic text is used to show the narrator of the last paragraph is not the same as the narrator of the rest of the text. **b)** Award **one** mark for correctly identifying that the narrator of this paragraph is the strange boy whom Casey sees. **c)** Award **one** mark for identifying two unusual words (from a choice of *sprite*, *maze-headed* and *frit*) and defining their meaning using inference from the surrounding text. For example: *'sprite' means a spirit or supernatural creature; 'maze-headed' means confused or imagining things; 'frit' means frightened.*	**3**
25. 2d 2e	Award **one** mark for any reasonable prediction based on evidence from the text. For example: *I think Casey and the boy will both get up early the next morning and come back to see if the other one is there. They will probably speak to each other this time, and make friends. The boy might take Casey hunting with him.*	**1**

13 questions, 20 marks

Section 3: The Fieldmouse – mark scheme

Question	Requirement	Mark
26. 2b	Award **one** mark for ticking the correct option: the fieldmouse ☑	**1**
27. 2b 2d	Award **two** marks for an answer that indicates it must be autumn or late summer, because of the falling acorns and berries and the long grass. Award **one** mark if the season is correctly identified but no reason is given.	**2**
28. 2b	Award **one** mark for an answer including one or both of the lines *'With your fur so soft and brown, With your eye so round and merry'*	**1**
29. 2a	**a)** Award **one** mark for a correct answer. For example: meaning hardly at all, barely or just, etc. **b)** Award **one** mark for an answer suggesting that the mouse moves so quickly and is so small it can be barely be seen.	**2**
30. 2a 2b	Award **one** mark for an answer explaining that the *treasure* it is the farmer's grain, crops or harvest, which are valuable to him because they help him make his living.	**1**

31. 2a 2d	**a)** Award **one** mark for ticking the correct option: crops ☑ **b)** Award **one** mark for an answer suggesting that the farmer has worked hard or suffered to harvest the corn. Evidence: '*But you must not steal the grain / He has stacked with so much pain.*'	**2**
32. 2a	Award **one** mark for the word crops.	**1**
33. 2a 2b	Award **one** mark for matching all answers correctly. Where does the fieldmouse sleep? *In what dark den* What does the fieldmouse eat? *Nibbling at their fallen fruits* Where shouldn't the fieldmouse go? *Where the farmer stacks his treasure* Where should the fieldmouse live? *Underneath the tall oak's shadow*	**1**
34. 2d	Award **one** mark for an answer suggesting that the fieldmouse might be in danger if it went too close to the corn or to the farmer's house. Evidence: '*Keep away from corn and house, / None will harm you, little mouse.*'	**1**
35. 2h	Award **two** marks for providing two appropriate phrases from the text. For example: A phrase that makes you think of the mouse as naughty is '*But you must not steal the grain*'; A phrase that makes you think of the mouse as good is '*Pretty, quiet, harmless thing*'.	**2**
36. 2g	Award **one** mark for a reasoned explanation of the student's opinion about the last two lines. For example: *Yes, I think they make a satisfying ending to the poem because they suggest a happy ending if the mouse does what the poet says, and the rhyming couplet at the end gives a sense of finality.*	**1**

11 questions, 15 marks

MARK SCHEME: GRAMMAR AND PUNCTUATION PRACTICE PAPER

This table shows you how marks are awarded for each of the questions in the grammar and punctuation test. The references in the 'Question' column (G3.4, G1.5a etc.) show you which aspects of the Content Domain are covered by each question.

The table includes guidance for each question to help you decide whether to award a mark or not. As a general point, when children need to write or complete a sentence in their answer, the sentence should be correctly punctuated and should not use capital letters other than the capital at the start of the sentence, except where proper nouns or the pronoun *I* are included in the sentence. If children make misspellings in their answers, you can still award the mark as long as the answer is otherwise correct, and as long as correct spelling is not the assessment focus of the question (e.g. when adding suffixes or prefixes to root words).

<table>
<tr><th>Question</th><th>Requirement</th><th>Mark</th></tr>
<tr><td>1.
G3.4</td><td>Award one mark for circling the correct word.

Tom kicked a stone along the pavement (while) he waited for his mum to finish shopping.</td><td>1</td></tr>
<tr><td>2.
G1.5 a, b</td><td>Award one mark for each sentence, for getting both pronouns correct.

When Lina's brothers saw <u>Lina</u> coming, <u>Lina's brothers</u> ran away.
Lina → her; Lina's brothers → they

Asif sat down on <u>Asif's</u> chair so fast that <u>Asif's chair</u> fell over.
Asif's → his; Asif's chair → it</td><td>2</td></tr>
<tr><td>3.
G5.11</td><td>Award one mark for ticking the correct option.

My dad loves fishing; he once caught a massive pike with razor-sharp teeth. ☑</td><td>1</td></tr>
<tr><td>4.
G5.7</td><td>Award one mark for a correctly completed table.

<table>
<tr><th>Sentence</th><th>Inverted commas used correctly</th><th>Inverted commas used incorrectly</th></tr>
<tr><td>"Listen, said Ola," "I've got something important to tell you."</td><td></td><td>✓</td></tr>
<tr><td>"Chocolate cake is my favourite, said Marco dreamily."</td><td></td><td>✓</td></tr>
<tr><td>"How many times do I have to tell you? said Mrs Fisher." Just sit down and wait quietly!</td><td></td><td>✓</td></tr>
<tr><td>"Deep in the heart of the jungle," said the guide, "there's a very rare white lion."</td><td>✓</td><td></td></tr>
</table></td><td>1</td></tr>
</table>

<table>
<tr><td>5.
G4.1c</td><td>Award one mark for circling the correct four words.

I might come round after tea today.
Do you think I should paint my bedroom black?
We will go and have lunch with Gran next Sunday.
Whatever you do, you must see the new spy film – it's amazing!</td><td></td></tr>
<tr><td>6.
G6.2</td><td>Award one mark for adding all four prefixes correctly.
misunderstand
disappear
untie
misbehave</td><td>1</td></tr>
<tr><td>7.
G2.1</td><td>Award one mark for ticking the correct option.

Far, far below the surface of the lake, something gigantic started to move. ☑</td><td>1</td></tr>
<tr><td>8.
G5.2</td><td>Award one mark for ticking the correct option.

full stop ☑</td><td>1</td></tr>
<tr><td>9.
G7.1</td><td>Award one mark for a correctly completed table.
<table>
<tr><th>Sentence</th><th>Standard English</th><th>non-Standard English</th></tr>
<tr><td>The sunflowers that we planted in the spring are taller than me now.</td><td>✓</td><td></td></tr>
<tr><td>The dog what stole our ball ran out of the park.</td><td></td><td>✓</td></tr>
<tr><td>Gran told me what she wanted from the shops.</td><td>✓</td><td></td></tr>
<tr><td>The bus what goes into town takes a really long time.</td><td></td><td>✓</td></tr>
</table></td><td>1</td></tr>
<tr><td>10.
G7.1</td><td>Award one mark for either of these responses:
Mum was tired, so I did all the washing up.
Mum was tired, so I have done all the washing up.</td><td>1</td></tr>
<tr><td>11.
G2.1</td><td>Award one mark for the response below, which must include a capital Y and a full stop.

You have finished eating your sandwich.</td><td>1</td></tr>
</table>

12. G2.1 G2.2 G2.3 G2.4	Award **one** mark for matching all correctly. 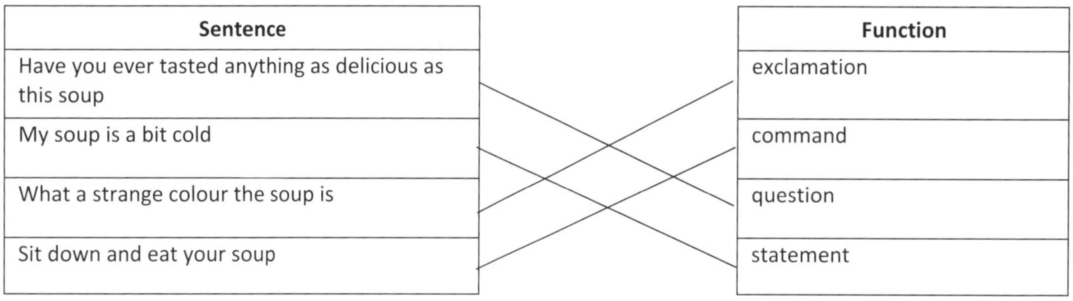	**1**
13. G1.6	Award **one** mark for any adverb that makes sense at the end of the sentence. For example: At home time, we all left the classroom quietly / noisily / quickly, etc. Do not award a mark for any sentence that does not use an adverb, or that uses an adverb that does not make sense in the sentence.	**1**
14. G1.3 G1.6	Award **one** mark for underlining and circling all words correctly. The slimy monster opened its enormous mouth hungrily, and its long green tentacles swung around wildly.	**1**
15. G1.4	Award **one** mark for all three conjunctions in the correct places. I got bored **while** I was waiting for Ali, **because** it took him ages to get changed, **so** I went home with Tom.	**1**
16. G1.8	Award **one** mark for writing all **four** determiners correctly. On my way home after school, I saw **a** massive dinosaur crossing the road. Mrs Fisher was riding on **the** dinosaur's back. She gave me **a** friendly wave. It was **an** amazing sight.	**1**
17. G1.5a	Award **one** mark for circling all **three** possessive pronouns correctly. Michael knew that he shouldn't have taken his sister's bike without asking her, but his bike had a puncture, and hers was just the right size for him to ride.	**1**
18. G3.4	Award **one** mark for underlining all **four** subordinate clauses correctly. We went to the park after we had finished all the shopping. Alex and I went swimming, while Mum and Nan sunbathed. After his exhausting day, Jamie went straight to bed. Because you kindly shared your crisps with me, I will give you a lick of my ice-cream.	**1**

<table>
<tr><td>19.
G3.3;
G3.4</td><td>Award one mark for correctly identifying all the conjunctions.
<table>
<tr><th>Sentence</th><th>Co-ordinating conjunction</th><th>Subordinating conjunction</th></tr>
<tr><td>We sat on the harbour wall and ate our fish and chips.</td><td>✓</td><td></td></tr>
<tr><td>The seagulls tried to steal our chips, but we scared them off.</td><td>✓</td><td></td></tr>
<tr><td>When we had finished our meal, we decided to go to the fairground.</td><td></td><td>✓</td></tr>
<tr><td>Jess regretted going on the big dipper, because she felt a bit sick.</td><td></td><td>✓</td></tr>
</table></td><td>1</td></tr>
<tr><td>20.
G3.2</td><td>Award one mark for underlining all noun phrases correctly and providing two appropriate adjectives to expand each one. For example:

<u>The dog</u> was growling. (enormous, hungry)
I've never seen such <u>a mess</u>! (gigantic, disgusting)
Fortunately, I had <u>a plan</u> (brilliant, daring)</td><td>1</td></tr>
<tr><td>21.
G6.4</td><td>Award one mark for ticking the correct option.
light ☑</td><td>1</td></tr>
<tr><td>22.
G4.1b</td><td>Award one mark for ticking both correct options.
Bella has lost her PE kit. ☑
Ted and Sanjit have spotted some baby birds in the nest in the big tree. ☑</td><td>1</td></tr>
<tr><td>23.
G4.1c</td><td>Award one mark for underlining all eight modal verbs correctly.

I <u>could</u> never dive from the top board – I <u>would</u> be too scared!
You <u>may</u> go swimming with Tom, but you <u>must</u> remember your goggles.
Rani <u>might</u> come to the cinema with us if she gets home in time.
You <u>should</u> let your little sister play, as otherwise she <u>might</u> start crying, and then your mum <u>would</u> get cross.</td><td>1</td></tr>
<tr><td>24.
G4.3</td><td>Award one mark for ticking the correct option ticked.
were ☑</td><td>1</td></tr>
<tr><td>25.
G6.1</td><td>Award one mark for correctly identifying all words.
Synonyms: tiny, minute, little, microscopic. Antonyms: enormous, gigantic, towering, huge.</td><td>1</td></tr>
<tr><td>26.
G6.2</td><td>Award one mark for a correct explanation of the difference in.
For example: Zac disarranged the cushions on the sofa. This means that Zac made the cushions look messy. Zac rearranged the cushions on the sofa. This means that Zac made the cushions look tidy again.</td><td>1</td></tr>
</table>

<table>
<tr><td>27.
G7.3</td><td>Award one mark for a sentence that has the same meaning as the original but uses some more formal language. For example:
I believe there are many children who would be delighted to receive an invitation to a swimming party.</td><td>1</td></tr>
<tr><td>28.
G5.1</td><td>Award one mark for completing the table correctly.
<table>
<tr><th>Sentence</th><th>Capitals used correctly</th><th>Capitals used incorrectly</th></tr>
<tr><td>After School on Wednesday we went to broadcliffe downs park.</td><td></td><td>✓</td></tr>
<tr><td>Martha and jamie have been friends since they were Five years old.</td><td></td><td>✓</td></tr>
<tr><td>Although I've never been to Paris, I've heard that the view from the top of the Eiffel Tower is amazing.</td><td>✓</td><td></td></tr>
<tr><td>We go to visit gran on Wednesdays and Fridays, but not usually at the Weekend.</td><td></td><td>✓</td></tr>
</table></td><td>1</td></tr>
<tr><td>29.
G5.5</td><td>Award one mark for correct punctuation as shown. Do not award the mark if commas are used after 'grapes' and 'water'.
At my party we ate pizza, garlic bread, carrot sticks, grapes and cake, and we drank lemonade, water and cola.</td><td>1</td></tr>
<tr><td>30.
G5.6b</td><td>Award one mark for a comma placed as shown.
Blotting out the sun with its magnificent wings, the dragon rose into the sky.</td><td>1</td></tr>
<tr><td>31.
G5.7</td><td>Award one mark for ticking the correct boxes.
☐ ☐
'I'm amazed you can manage a piece of cake after all that pizza,' said Grandad admiringly.</td><td>1</td></tr>
<tr><td>32.
G5.9</td><td>Award one mark for ticking the correct option.
In the cupboard under the stairs, just behind the vacuum cleaner, lived a tiny goblin. ☑</td><td>1</td></tr>
<tr><td>33.
G1.7</td><td>Award one mark for circling all three prepositions.
(Before) Mina tiptoed (across) the empty hallway, she peered cautiously (through) the gap in the door</td><td>1</td></tr>
<tr><td>34.
G1.6a</td><td>Award one mark for underlining the correct phrase.
When I said I didn't like football, Tomas looked at me <u>as if I was mad</u>.</td><td>1</td></tr>
<tr><td>35.
G1.9</td><td>Award one mark for circling the subject circled and underlining the object correctly.
(The soldier) stood on <u>the castle battlements</u>.</td><td>1</td></tr>
<tr><td>36.
G3.1a</td><td>Award one mark for ticking the two correct options.
Grandad, whose garden is his pride and joy, is brilliant at growing roses. ☑
The garden, which is overshadowed by trees at one end, is a lovely place to play in. ☑</td><td>1</td></tr>
</table>

37. G3.1; G3.4	Award **one** mark identifying the correct clauses in each case. Main clauses: I've never liked fishcakes; Marek asked if he could sit at my table. Subordinate clauses: Digging about underneath the brambles and nettles; When you open the present.	1
38. G4.1a	Award **one** mark for circling the correct words. We (went) to the cinema on Saturday, but unfortunately the film (was) rubbish.	1
39. G4.1a	Award **one** mark for accurately transposing the sentence into the present tense. For example: Dominic tries his very best, but he can't catch up with Malia.	1
40. G4.2	Award **one** mark for circling the correct verb and writing the correct past tense form. Mattie woke with a start, leapt up from the bed and (shoots) downstairs to the front door. <u>Shot</u>	1
41. G4.4	Award **one** mark for a sentence that expresses the same meaning using the passive voice. For example: Most of the glass in the greenhouse was broken by Maia's football.	1
42. G5.10	Award **one** mark for a colon in the correct place. I've had a brilliant idea: I'm going to build my own space rocket.	1
43. G6.1	Award **one** mark for an appropriate word with the opposite meaning to those underlined. For example: delicious: disgusting; enjoy: dislike; chilly: warm; helpful: unhelpful	1
44. G5.13	Award **one** mark for an accurate description of the difference in meaning. For example: The pet shop has five <u>year-old</u> rabbits means that the pet shop has five rabbits that are a year old. The pet shop has <u>five-year-old</u> rabbits means that the pet shop has rabbits that are five years old.	1
45. G5.12	Award **one** mark for ticking the correct option. We all enjoyed the holiday – even Daniel, who got stung by a wasp. ☑	1
46. G5.11	Award **one** mark for a semi-colon in the correct place. We're going to have salad for tea; it's far too hot to have soup.	1
47. G6.3	Award **one** mark for adding appropriate suffixes to all the root words. For example: helpful or helpless; comfortable or comfortless; peaceful or peaceable; careful or careless.	1
48. G5.6a	Award **one** mark for correct placement of the commas. The children, who had been good all term, got a special treat.	1
49. G5.8	Award **one** mark for correct placement of the apostrophes. The women's changing room wasn't in use that day, because there were decorators' ladders and paint pots everywhere.	1

49 questions, 50 marks

Spelling script

1. The word is **enjoyable**.
Dad cooked a very __enjoyable__ meal.
The word is **enjoyable**.

2. The word is **special**.
Gran's dog has a __special__ blanket to sleep on.
The word is **special**.

3. The word is **advice**.
I would like to ask your __advice__ about something.
The word is **advice**.

4. The word is **restaurant**.
The __restaurant__ was full of people enjoying their meal.
The word is **restaurant**.

5. The word is **eight**.
Our rabbits had __eight__ babies.
The word is **eight**.

6. The word is **gymnastics**.
I like doing __gymnastics__, but I'm not very good at cartwheels.
The word is **gymnastics**.

7. The word is **chef**.
The __chef__ put plenty of pepper in the stew.
The word is **chef**.

8. The word is **younger**.
Sasha is two years __younger__ than me.
The word is **younger**.

9. The word is **television**.
Grandad fell asleep in front of the __television__.
The word is **television**.

10. The word is **knights.**
At the castle we saw some __knights__ jousting.
The word is **knights.**

11. The word is **responsibly**.
"I'll look after you," said Jack __responsibly__.
The word is **responsibly**.

12. The word is **important**.
Mum gave Stefan a very __important__ job.
The word is **important**.

13. The word is **immature**.
Rob is eighteen, but he is rather __immature__.
The word is **immature**.

14. The word is **precious**.
Let me show you my most __precious__ possession.
The word is **precious**.

15. The word is **exaggeration**.
Sam said he could swim, but that was an __exaggeration__.
The word is **exaggeration**.

16. The word is **choir.**
The __choir__ sang beautifully.
The word is **choir.**

17. The word is **helpfully**.
Aneeta __helpfully__ cleared the table.
The word is **helpfully**.

18. The word is **tongue**.
It hurt when I bit my __tongue__.
The word is **tongue**.

19. The word is **cough**.
Dad has a nasty __cough__ today.
The word is **cough**.

20. The word is **communication**.
Text messages are a quick method of __communication__.
The word is **communication**.

MARK SCHEME: SPELLING PRACTICE PAPER

The spellings covered in this test are taken from the curriculum requirements for Years 5 and 6, and include examples of most of the required spelling patterns. The mark scheme below shows the correct spelling for each word featured in the test.

Question	Spelling	Mark	Content domain reference
1	enjoyable	1	S38, S56 - adding suffixes beginning with vowel letters to words of more than one syllable; words ending in *–able* and *–ible*
2	special	1	S44 - words with endings sounding like */ʒə/* or */tʃə/*
3	advice	1	S61 - homophones and other words that are often confused
4	restaurant	1	S37, S55 - common exception words; words ending in *–ant, –ance, –ancy, –ent, –ence, –ency*
5	eight	1	S52 - words with the */eɪ/* sound spelled *ei, eigh,* or *ey*
6	gymnastics	1	S39 - words with the */i/* sound spelled *y* other than at the end of words
7	chef	1	S49 - words with the */ʃ/* sound spelled *ch*
8	younger	1	S40 - words with the */ʌ/* sound spelled *ou*
9	television	1	S47 - words with endings that sound like */ʃən/,* spelled *–tion, –sion, –ssion, –cian*
10	knights	1	S60 - words with 'silent' letters (i.e. letters whose presence cannot be predicted from the pronunciation of the word)
11	responsibly	1	S38 - adding suffixes beginning with vowel letters to words of more than one syllable
12	important	1	S55 - words ending in *–ant, –ance, –ancy, –ent, –ence, –ency*
13	immature	1	S41 - prefixes
14	precious	1	S53 - words with endings which sound like */ʃəs/* spelled –cious or –tious
15	exaggeration	1	S42 - the suffix *–ation*
16	choir	1	S48 - words with the */k/* sound spelled *ch*
17	helpfully	1	S43 - the suffix *–ly*
18	tongue	1	S50 - words ending with the */g/* sound spelled *–gue* and the */k/* sound spelled *–que*
19	cough	1	S59 - words containing the letter string *ough*
20	communication	1	S37 - common exception words
	Total	**20**	

Published by Pearson Education Limited, 80 Strand, London, WC2R 0RL.

www.pearsonschools.co.uk

Series consultant: Margaret Reeve
Edited by Elektra Media Ltd
Designed by Andrew Magee
Typeset by Elektra Media Ltd
Produced by Elektra Media Ltd

Illustrated by Elektra Media Ltd
Cover design by Andrew Magee

First published 2016

19 18 17 16
10 9 8 7 6 5 4 3 2 1

British Library Cataloguing in Publication Data
A catalogue record for this book is available from the British Library

ISBN 978 1 292 17250 7

Printed in the United Kingdom by Ashford Colour Press Ltd

Acknowledgements

We would like to thank Tutora for its invaluable help in the development and trialling of this course.

We are grateful to the following for permission to reproduce copyright material:

Text
Poetry on page 14 'It's Spring' (Foster, J,) from *The Works*, Pan Macmillan, p183; copyright © John Foster, by permission of the author. Poetry on page 14 'How the Tortoise Got Its Shell' (Nicholls, J.) from *The Works*, Pan Macmillan, p57; copyright © 2000 Judith Nicholls, by permission of the author.